George Chalmers, Charles J. Fox

Defence of Opposition With Respect to Their Conduct on Irish Affairs

With explanatory notes

George Chalmers, Charles J. Fox

Defence of Opposition With Respect to Their Conduct on Irish Affairs
With explanatory notes

ISBN/EAN: 9783337124687

Printed in Europe, USA, Canada, Australia, Japan

Cover: Foto ©Suzi / pixelio.de

More available books at **www.hansebooks.com**

DEFENCE OF OPPOSITION

WITH RESPECT TO

THEIR CONDUCT

ON

IRISH AFFAIRS,

WITH

EXPLANATORY NOTES.

DEDICATED

TO THE RIGHT HONOURABLE

C. J. FOX.

BY AN IRISH GENTLEMAN,
A MEMBER OF THE WHIG CLUB.

LONDON:
PRINTED FOR JOHN STOCKDALE,
OPPOSITE BURLINGTON-HOUSE, PICCADILLY.
M DCC LXXXV.

TO THE

Right Hon. C. J. FOX.

SIR,

THE founding a commercial intercourse between Great-Britain and Ireland, upon the basis of mutual advantage, seems a measure so wise, and salutary in itself, and so promising in its consequences, as naturally to excite a more than ordinary share of the public attention.

The object has long had the warmest wishes of the best, and most exalted characters of both countries, and the most fervent prayers of every one not insensible of their welfare and happiness; and it is with inexpressible pleasure and satisfaction, they now behold it ripening, and nearly brought to a state of maturity, by the fostering hand of the present most excellent Minister, who, with his father's resplendent virtues, most happily blends the wisdom of age and experience.

A measure, Sir, that will at once do away all those jealousies that have so long filled the breast of Ireland—that must for ever attach her to Great-Britain—and make their interest one and the same, cannot but claim a very powerful support from the representatives of the people.

It is, therefore, with much surprize, the public hear, that you, and those you are in the habit of voting with, (including your *new* friends) intend to give it every opposition in your power.

The *consistency* of your conduct, in the line of politics, gives, at once, the flattest contradiction to so impudent and barefaced a calumny.

The following sheets, however, will effectually put the matter out of doubt, and do you ample justice.

They are the faithful extracts of various speeches delivered in Parliament by *you*, and *those* you have the honor to act with, and will be found to contain the strongest recommendations of the *very* measures, now under discussion, for establishing a fair and equal trade between Great-Britain and Ireland.

You will please, therefore, to accept of them as the best, and most conclusive refutation of the charges brought against you, as from them, it is impossible, considering how very unlikely *you* are to be actuated by party views, that the minister can want *your* support and assistance.

I have the honor to be,

SIR,

Your most devoted humble servant,

A MEMBER OF THE WHIG CLUB.

ST. ALBAN'S TAVERN,
 March 19, 1785.

CONTENTS.

	Page
Mr. Sawbridge	1
Mr. Burke	1
———	4
———	18
Lord Beauchamp	1
———	2
———	18
———	27
Earl of Upper Ossory	2
Mr. Fox	5
———	12
———	14
———	15
———	26
———	28
Lord North	6
———	7
———	11
Mr. Welbore Ellis	6
Lord George Germaine	7
Mr. Eden	11
———	19
———	28
Mr. Sheridan	13
Mr. Fitzpatrick	15
———	26
Gen. Burgoyne	17
Earl of Hilsborough	31
———	34
———	38
Earl Gower	35
Earl of Carlisle	37
Duke of Portland	39

CONTENTS

OF THE

APPENDIX.

I. THE COMMERCIAL RESOLUTIONS of the IRISH PARLIAMENT in their present Session VINDICATED, to which is added an AUTHENTIC COPY of the RESOLUTIONS   Page 1

I. A SHORT VIEW of the Proposals lately made for the FINAL ADJUSTMENT of the COMMERCIAL SYSTEM between GREAT-BRITAIN and IRELAND — — — Page 13

III. THE ARRANGEMENTS with IRELAND CONSIDERED — — Page 21

IV. CONSIDERATIONS, respecting the ARRANGEMENTS with IRELAND — — Page 59

HOUSE OF COMMONS.

Mr. SAWBRIDGE.

I Am againſt all monopolies of trade, and commercial interdictions; there is trade enough for every nation upon earth, *if all impolitic reſtrictions were repealed.* No nation, nor corporate body, nor individual, has a right to deprive another *of the benefits of manufactures, trade, and commerce.*
March 18, 1779[*].

Mr. BURKE.

It is for the *intereſt* of Great Briain to throw open *even the woollen trade to Ireland*; and if it is not done now voluntarily, the French will ſoon oblige us to do it. March 18, 1779.

Lord BEAUCHAMP.

The language the noble Lord, (Earl of Hilſborough) uſed in the other Houſe of the late miniſters, (Lord North, &c.) clearly meant an equality of export

---

[*] The order of the day was for going into a committee on the importation of ſugars into Ireland, which was loſt on a diviſion, 62 to 53.

export and import duties, customs, &c. an equality of trade, and consequently of mutual advantage. *Nov.* 30, 1779.

Earl of UPPER OSSORY.

As an Irishman, and bound to Ireland by the strongest ties of interest and affection, it might be fairly, and I will add, be truly presumed, that I entertain the most sincere wishes for her happiness and prosperity; nay, I will say, that as an Englishman, it is my duty to do so, because I am persuaded, *that whatever promotes the trade and commerce of* Ireland, *will ultimately promote that of* Great Britain. *Dec.* 6, 1779.

Lord BEAUCHAMP.

That Ireland is in a distressed situation, no man within or without this House will, I dare say, venture to deny; but I can never be persuaded to think, that the miseries which Ireland feels, and under which she at present groans, can be fairly attributed to the present ministry; or indeed to any ministry within my remembrance. The grievance has not originated, at least since the present reign, with any particular set of men in power, nor from any recent measures adopted in respect to that country. The causes are various, *but the prime source* of the distresses of that kingdom, *is the system of our trade laws,* which lay *a restraint upon*

upon her commerce. I am convinced, that thefe reftrictions arife from a very narrow, fhort-fighted policy, conceived in prejudice, and ftrengthened by time; which, after more than a century, has been wrought, as it were, into the very conftitution of this country.

For my own part, I think *the intereft of both countries is infeparable,* as their political connexion is indiffoluble, and whoever endeavours to obftruct either, *is no friend to his country,* that is, *he is ignorant of the true profperity of both**.

Though enjoying a place under the Crown, my fituation is not fuch, as to entitle me to know what paffes in his Majefty's council; but I have heard in converfation, that the noble Lord on the fame bench, (Lord *North*) in concert with the reft of his Majefty's fervants, have agreed upon propofitions, which are to be fubmitted to this houfe. I am ignorant of their purport; but from what I heard fall from a noble Lord (Earl of Hilfborough) in the other houfe, the firft day of the feffion; to whom, both England, and Ireland, owe the higheft obligations, it is fuppofed, *that Ireland will be*

---

* As neither Lord *North,* Mr. *Fox,* nor Mr. *Burke,* can be thought *ignorant* of the true profperity of both England and Ireland, according to Lord *Beauchamp,* neither of them *is a friend to his country;* and they will hardly have the ill manners to contradict a noble Lord they fo cordially act with.

be granted an equal trade, or an equality of trade, upon the broad basis, of impartiality and justice.

Dec. 6, 1779.

Mr. BURKE.

Ireland spurns at the British claim of dominion: she looks upon herself *free and independent*, and is firmly determined to maintain it. The American war originated in injustice, has been conducted with cruelty, and is likely to end in infamy, disgrace, and disappointment. The loyalty of the people of Ireland can no more procure justice at the hands of ministers, than the stubborn spirit of America. Ireland, driven to the last stage of human misery and distress, is left to her wretched fate; she intreats—she supplicates—but in vain. Without a pretence of offence on her part, she is left to her fate, unattended to, and unpitied!

Ireland now will not be satisfied *with any thing short of a free trade*. The people of Ireland have reasoned fairly and justly: the colonies, they know, have been offered the most that their own most sanguine expectations could aspire to, a free trade with all the world. America, for her revolt, has had a choice of favours held out to her: This is the reward of rebellion. Ireland for her loyalty, for almost a century, and her forbearance under accumulated oppression, and internal distresses, has been refused the mighty indulgence of importing her own sugars; at all events, without taking

taking any peculiar merit with the British Government, for their loyal, faithful, and peaceable demeanor, they thought they were at least entitled to meet the colonies upon equal terms, and with equal expectations of favor and relief to those which America has spurned at with contempt.

I am induced, from every consideration, which strikes me, to believe, *that whatever measure will serve Ireland essentially, will, and must, in the end, serve England.*   Dec. 6, 1779.

Mr. F O X.

It is the general calamities of the empire, that has made Ireland *poor*; but it is the incapacity and negligence of goverment, that has rendered her bold and daring. It is therefore incumbent upon parliament, to shew their fullest disapprobation of that indolence and incapacity; and convince Ireland, that they are as ready as themselves to resent and punish the cruel and improper treatment, which they have received from ministers. Ireland will see by such a conduct, thas it is not this country, but its ministers who are blameable, which will, in my opinion, prove the surest means of once more binding both countries in the strongest, and most indissoluble ties of friendship and affection.   Dec. 6, 1779.

Lord

Lord NORTH.

Many favors have been granted to Ireland, since I have had the honour of a seat in his Majesty's councils, such as the free importation of beef and butter rendered perpetual; the encouragement given to the Newfoundland cod fishery; and the Southern whale fishery, by bounties granted by the British parliament; the giving leave to export woollen for clothing the troops on the Irish establishment, serving out of that kingdom; the act for encouraging the culture of tobacco and hemp, by permitting its importation into Great Britain; the permission of the export of several enumerated articles to the British sugar colonies, and the coast of Africa, &c. These favors, howsoever liberally given, have not answered, nor proved sufficiently efficacious in removing the difficulties the people of Ireland labour under, *from the restrictions laid upon her trade, nor the distresses that are the consequences of those restrictions* What parliament may do, is not for me to foretell, nor dictate; but I presume, they will come with the best dispositions towards their brethren in Ireland, *and grant them every thing which does not apparently clash with the essential interests of this kingdom.* Dec. 6, 1779.

Mr. WELBORE ELLIS.

Though a native of Ireland, I rise as a member of this house, to give my opinion, relative to the interest

interest of my constituents, and am happy to find myself in a situation, when I can unite a strict discharge of my duty with my native feelings. *The interest* of Great Britain and Ireland *are reciprocal and mutual.* *Dec.* 6, 1779.

Lord GEO. GERMAINE.

Persons of great weight and ability in this kingdom have been consulted on the subject of our differences with Ireland, but their opinions were so contradictory, that no certain information, or what would promise to give satisfaction, could be obtained, sufficient to ground measures upon, and consequently neither Ministry, nor Parliament could decide, *till a proper specification was made by the People of Ireland*, through the only channel on which it could be relied on, or attended to. That specification has been made; the Irish Parliament have come to an unanimous vote, *that nothing short of a free trade would answer the object* which their present situation necessarily points to. The Irish Parliament has been explicit, *and I hope that their desires will be granted* *.

Dec. 6, 1779.

Lord NORTH.

I mean now to open my three propositions, relative to the allowing Ireland a free export of her

---

* Nothing can possibly be more agreeable to this, than the conduct observed by the present minister towards Ireland.

her wool, woollens, and wool flocks; a free exportation of glafs, and of all kinds of glafs manufactures; of a freedom of trade with the Britifh plantations, on certain conditions, the bafis of which is to be *an equality of taxes and cuftoms, upon an equal and unreftrained trade.*

To demonftrate the matter of right, as well as favour, I beg leave to ftate the two following propofitions: Firft, *That Ireland has a free and unlimited right to trade with the whole world.* Secondly, That Ireland does not, nor cannot, pretend to claim any right, directly, or co-relatively, with any part of the Britifh colonies, or plantations. Every perfon in both kingdoms, muft inftantly give an univerfal affent to the latter propofition. It is not my wifh to enter into a difcuffion of the former, or debate points merely fpeculatively: fo much, however, I will hazard, that mixing the broad claim of a free and unreftrained trade, and qualifying it with the advantage derivable from a connection with Great-Britain, it will not be too much to fay, that although the claim is with Ireland, the option of a connexion with this country, and a participation of commercial intereft, *is clearly in favor of Great-Britain.*

It is both the intereft, and inclination of Ireland, to ftand well with England, and on the idea of fuch a natural and political connexion; they have been rather harfhly and impolitically treated:

before

before the Restoration they enjoyed every commercial advantage and benefit in common with England.

The commerce, import and export, was held in common by both kingdoms till the reign of Charles the Second: even the act of navigation, the great foundation of our plantation laws, put England and Ireland upon exact terms of equality; nor was it till two years after that the first commercial restriction was laid on Ireland, and that not directly, but by a side wind, and by deductive interpretation. When the act first passed, there was a general governing clause, for giving bonds to perform the conditions of the act, but then the act was amended, in the fifteenth of Charles the Second: whence a conclusion was drawn, that the acts of the two preceding Parliaments, twelfth, thirteenth, and fourteenth of Charles the Second, were thereby repealed, though it was as clearly expressed in these acts, as it was possible for words to convey, that ships built in Ireland, *navigated with the people thereof*, were deemed British, and quialfied to trade to and from the British plantations; and that ships built in Ireland, and navigated with his Majesty's subjects of Ireland, *were entitled to the same abatements and privileges, to which importers and exporters of goods in British built ships were entitled by the book of rates*.

Upon an average of the six years, from 1766 to 1772, the export to Ireland was something more than two millions; and in the succeeding six years,

C ending

ending in 1778, about as much more, one half nearly British manufacture or produce, the other half certificated articles, of which this country was the medium of conveyance; out of the native produce, which was something more than 900,000l. per annum, on the average, only 200,000 were woollens: so that in this light, supposing every thing that any man could wish to conclude from the fact, I must submit to the House, whether it would be found policy to risque *a million export* of native produce, for a woollen export of 200,000l.

The woollen manufacture must, indeed, a long time continue in a state of infancy; and though cloths have been manufactured sufficient to answer a considerable part of the home consumption, yet it can hardly be expected that Ireland will be able to rival Great Britain at the foreign markets, when, after the expence of land carriage, freight, insurance, factorage, &c. she is able to undersell Ireland in her own markets on the very spot, though aided by the advantage of low wages and taxes.

Should the Irish be permitted to enjoy a free export of woollens, I should still be for continuing the bounties paid on the importation into England of certain species of fabrics of Irish Linens.

The subject demands much consideration, and requires much modelling. It is a matter of infinite delicacy, and will call for a great deal of detail and enquiry, and therefore ought not to be hurried on.

Though

Though under different legiflatures, Great-Britain and Ireland *have but one conjugal intereft*; and are, in the general fenfe of the phrafe, BUT ONE PEOPLE. Even fhould fhe (Ireland) be enabled to rival us in foreign markets, in a few commodities of native growth, cheapnefs of labour, and other incidental circumftances, we fhould not forget *that Ireland forms a part of the Britifh Empire.*

Dec. 13, 1779.

Lord NORTH.

In one article of Importation, viz. *that of fugar,* Ireland may probably ftill choofe to take them *circuitoufly* through England, at the low duties, in preference to *directly* importing them at the high duties. *Jan.* 24, 1780.

Mr. EDEN.

Will it not be expedient to anticipate the wifhes of Ireland, and convince her of our fincere intentions, to give her every fecurity in our power for the permanency of her conftitution, and of that trade which fhe is fo anxious to preferve? *

April 18, 1782.

Mr.

---

* On the 2d of February, 1785, the following Refolutions were *unanimoufly* agreed to, viz. to allow the exporting, carrying or conveying *corn* out of this realm into Ireland; to admit *foreign hops* there; and to repeal the acts which take off *the drawbacks on Britifh hops*; and for the Irifh to be admitted *to the Turkey Company*, &c. No oppofition was given to thefe Refolutions, nor any debate had thereon.

Mr. FOX.[*]

The disposition of the King's ministers towards Ireland, I believe, is sufficiently understood; and that disposition, which they have expressed, *when out of office*, I sincerely believe they will now maintain, and will take the speeediest and most likely means of giving *compleat satisfaction to the people of Ireland*.

I trust in the candor of the House, for the confidence which they will have in the intentions of his Majesty's Ministers towards Ireland; and that they will believe that they mean and wish most ardently to bring the matter forward in the most speedy manner. I will again assure them, that it has always been my political sentiment, that it is unjust and tyrannical to attempt to hold a country in subjection, and to govern against the will and opinion of the people. It has always been my sentiments with regard to America, as well as Ireland, that they cannot, much less ought not to be governed by laws which they reject as unconstitutional. All just Government must consist in the perfect consent, good will, and opinion of the people; it is the best and surest system of Government where harmony prevails; and without it, it is not Government, but *usurpation*.

It

---

[*] At this time one of his Majesty's principal Secretaries of State.

It is certainly the most consistent with true policy, as well as justice, to bring about a final settlement of the dispute between Great Britain and Ireland; to state, and precisely to declare, *not for a moment*, but for ever, what is the relative situation of the two countries with respect to each other; to take in and conclude all the points of difference, and to establish such a *system* of connexion, intimacy, and relation between them, as shall be immediately, and permanently, for the interest of both. To be settled for ages, and not, as has been the conduct of late ministers, sear up the wound for a moment, without compleating the cure. When those ministers agreed to the extension of the trade with Ireland, they should have ultimately settled the claim, and fixed the situation. They failed to do this at the proper time, and they ought to answer for it to their country: *that measures however will be used for accomplishing this desirable end, I may safely assure the house.** I think that deceit is always pernicious, and I wish to speak with as much openness, and information, as the nature of my office can justify.

April 8, 1782.

Mr. SHERIDAN.

The attack made by the Honourable Gentleman (Mr. Eden) on the new ministers, is scandalously unfair

---

* What *but this*, is Mr. *Fox*, and his party, *now* opposing in the House of Commons?—

unfair, *as I am convinced that they* * *have the fairest intentions towards Ireland.* April 8, 1782.

Mr. FOX.

His Majesty is most earnestly desirous of settling the discontents and jealousies that subsist in the minds of his subjects of the kingdom of Ireland. The measures which his Majesty's ministers conceive necessary to be taken in the present instance, and which I am to propose to the House, *will require a great deal of most serious discussion.* The House will perceive, that in the pretensions of the Irish, expressed by the parliament and people, that the matter contains no less than the constitution of the kingdom, that it comprehends not only the commercial rights, and privileges of the kingdom, but also the legislative power and royalty. The most important objects are therefore embraced, and both nations are most materially concerned, in the discussion and settlement of the matter: they are topics, upon which they will see his Majesty cannot decide, without the assistance of his parliament; nor *indeed without the assistance and concurrence of both parliaments.* To come to the business therefore with propriety, and in a manner that will give effect to their proceedings, they must have full and authentic

---

* Meaning, no doubt, Lord *North*, Mr. *Fox*, &c.

authentic information; *and both parliaments must take time in their deliberation.**   *April* 4, 1782.

Hon. Colonel FITZPATRICK.

I have been prevailed upon to accept of the office of the Secretary of the Lord Lieutenant of Ireland, in the firm persuasion and confidence, that his *Majesty's present ministers*† are sincere in their professions; and that THEY are earnestly disposed to make such concessions to Ireland, as shall quiet their jealousies, and give satisfaction to their minds. If I had not had this opinion of the King's Ministers, no circumstance on earth should have induced me to take a situation which at any time I would not have coveted, *and which only such opinion and confidence would make me endure.* It is the wise policy of this country, to make those concessions, as from the establishment of a firm and friendly relation, founded upon clear, and known constitution, *the most happy consequences wi'l be derived to both countries.*   *April* 9, 1, 82.

Mr. FOX.

Ireland, may perhaps think of fresh grievances, and rise yearly in her demands; it is fit and proper therefore, that something should be now done towards establishing on a firm and solid basis,

the

---

* Every possible information has been sought after by the *present minister*, and time given *for the fullest deliberation* on the subject of Irish affairs.

† Lord *North*, Mr. *Fox*, &c.

the future connexion of the two kingdoms; but that is to be proposed by me here in parliament; it will be the duty of the Crown to look to that; *the business may be first begun by his Majesty's servants in Ireland* *; and if afterwards it shall be necessary to enter into a treaty, commissioners may be sent from the British parliament or from the Crown, to enter upon it, and to bring the negotiation to a happy issue, by giving mutual satisfaction to both countries, and establishing a treaty, which shall be sanctified by the most solemn forms of the constitution of both countries.

I have no doubt, but that in affection, as well as in *interest*, Ireland and Great-Britain will be *but one people*. If any man should entertain any gloomy ideas on the subject, let him look at the concluding paragraph of the Irish addresses; where he will find, that the Irish people and parliament *are filled with the most earnest desires to support England*, to have the same enemy and the same friend; in a word, *to stand or fall with England*. Let gentlemen look forward to that happy period, when Ireland shall experience the blessings, *that attend freedom of trade and constitution*; when by the richness and fertility of her soil, the industry of her manufacturers, and the encrease of her population, she shall become a powerful country; then

may

---

* Surely Mr. *Pitt* cannot but be considered as extremely fortunate, in having proceeded in a manner, *so strongly recommended by Mr.* FOX.

may England look for powerful affiftance in feamen to man her fleets, and foldiers to fight her battles.

England renouncing all right to legiflate for Ireland, the latter will moft cordially fupport the former, as a friend whom fhe loves; if this country, on the one hand, is to affume the power of making laws for Ireland, fhe will only make an enemy inftead of a friend; *for where there is a community of intereft* *, and a mutual regard for thofe interefts, there the party whofe interefts are facrificed becomes an enemy.

Upon the whole, I am convinced that the Irifh defire nothing more ardently, *than proper grounds for being moft cordially united to England*, and I am fure that they will be attached to this country *even to bigotry*. May 17, 1782.

General BURGOYNE.

I cannot prevail upon myfelf to give a filent vote; the great revolution that has been effected, with fo much calmnefs and fteadinefs, does the higheft honour to Ireland; and I cannot exprefs myfelf better in praife of the characters who have effected it, upon the greateft principles of freedom, than in the words of the Roman author, *eos qui de nihilo nifi libertate cogitant, dignos effe qui Romani fiant.* Thofe who know how to think fo juftly of it, *deferve to be free*. . May 17, 1782.

B Lord

---

* Such a one as the *prefent* minifter propofes to eftablifh.

Lord BEAUCHAMP.

It is not the mere repeal of the 6 Geo. 1. that will satisfy Ireland, because the repeal will leave the question just as it was before. *May* 17, 1782.

Mr. BURKE.

It is not on such a day as this, when there is not a difference of opinion*, that I will rise to fight the battle of Ireland; *her cause is nearest my heart,* and nothing gave me so much satisfaction, when I was first honoured with a seat in this House, as it might be in my power, *some way or other, to be of service to the country that gave me birth* †; and I have always said to myself, that if such an insignificant member as I am, can ever be so fortunate as to render an essential service to England, and that my sovereign, or parliament, were going to reward me for it, I would say to them—*do something for Ireland—do something for my country, and I am over-rewarded*——I am a friend to my country, but gentlemen need not be jealous of that; for in being

the

---

* Respecting the repeal of the 6 of Geo. 1.

† There surely then can be but little doubt of the minister's having Mr. *Burke's* support in carrying his commercial regulations, between Great Britain and Ireland, through this House.

the friend of Ireland, I deem myself of course the friend of England—*their interests are inseparable.*

May 17, 1782.*

Mr. EDEN†.

It was wisdom in the Irish Parliaament to chuse an undefined expression upon a subject so complicated and extensive in all its connexions and consequences; the whole consideration is now opened to both kingdoms, *and it is the interest of both to come to an early kind of efficient conclusion*‡.

It is a political truth, that happiness and strength should be extended *through the constituent parts of an Empire,* as far as wise and beneficial laws can operate to that effect. It would next be easy to shew, that public happiness and strength are diffused in proportion to the plenty and convenience with which not only the natural wants of a people are supplied, but such adventitious ones as are superinduced by universal habit and industry: when this end is not attained to a certain degree, an Empire may

---

* Mr. *Fox* on this day moved, that it is the opinion of this committee (the House being then in a committee) that the interests of Great Britain and Ireland *are inseparable,* and that their connexion *ought to be founded on a solid and permanent basis,* to which the committee agreed without a debate.

† See his letter, entitled, A Letter on the Representations of Ireland, respecting a Free Trade.

‡ Page 140.

may indeed exist, and may encreafe in numbers, but it will grow like an unwieldy body, liable to dangers and acute humours*.

Whatever may have been the syftem of government adopted, or accepted by Ireland, the recent and moft interefting fact is, that fhe now complains of fome diftreffes which fhe conceives to refult from that fyftem. Thefe diftreffes are poffibly no more than have refulted from temporary caufes;—from the late rebellion with the Colonies, or from the calamities incident to war; but we know perfectly, that the complaint is founded in real fufferings. The firft inference which would arife from this fact, in any mind reafoning kindly towards a part of the Empire, and difcreetly in refpect of the whole, *is, that the Irifh, as fellow fubjects, are intitled to every relief compatible with the general interefts*†.

If we were to ftate to an Irifh gentleman, the long continued poverty and idlenefs whichhave prevailed over fo large a proportion of his countrymen, he would probably anfwer——

" All this may be true, but the monopolizing
" fpirit of our fifter kingdom is the caufe of it:
" that fpirit exercifing itfelf upon Ireland in a
" very early ftate of her civilization, nipped her
dif-

* Page 142.   † Page 143.

" disposition to industry, and, indeed, made it im-
" possible for her to become industrious. In the
" very infancy of our country, and whilst we were
" contenting ourselves with the exportations and
" sale of our cattle, you made an act * to pro-
" hibit those exportations. We next gave our
" attention to the increase of our sheep, in order
" to export wool, but you forthwith † prohibited
" the exportation of wool, and made it subject to
" forfeiture. We then endeavoured to employ
" and support ourselves by salting provisions for
" sale; but you immediately ‡ refused them ad-
" mittance into England, in order to encrease the
" rents of your lands, though you thereby en-
" creased the wages of your labourers. We next
" began a woollen manufacture; but it was no
" sooner established than destroyed; for you
" prohibited § the exportation of manufactured
" woollens to any other place than England and
" Wales, and this prohibition alone is reported to
" have forced twenty thousand manufacturers out
" of the kingdom.

" The Navigation Act ‖ had unwittingly, but
" kindly, permitted all commodities to be imported
" into Ireland, upon the same terms as into Eng-
" land: but by an act ** passed three years after-
" wards,

* 8 Eliz. ch. 3.   † 13 and 14 Car. II. ch. 18.
‡ 18 Car. II. ch. 2.   § 10 and 11 Will. III. ch. 10.
‖ 12 Car. II. ch. 10.   ** 10 and 11 Will. III. ch. 10.

" wards, the exportation of any goods from Ire-
" land into any of the plantations was prohibited:
" and as if that had not sufficiently crippled the
" benefits given by the Navigation Act, we were
" soon * afterwards forbid to import any of the
" enumerated commodities from the plantations
" into Ireland. This restriction too was much
" enforced by subsequent acts, and the list of enu-
" merated goods was much encreased. I say no-
" thing of your regulations respecting glass, hops,
" sail-cloth, &c. † and other inferior barriers and
" obstructions to our commerce: we subsisted
" under all this, and under a drain also, which
" has gradually encreased upon us, by remittances
" to our own absentees, English mortgages, Go-
" vernment annuitants, and other extra-commer-
" cial purposes, to the amount of half a million
" sterling annually. And though we retained no
" trade but in linen, and provisions, the latter has
" been under a three years prohibition, during
" which period we lost the principal market for
" our own beef, though three-fourths of our peo-
" ple were graziers. Many of us, indeed, carried
" on a clandestine trade, and it was essential to
" our support; but that too has been lately check-
" ed, first by the revolt of the colonies, and now
" by the war with France and Spain.

" Our

* 22 Car. II. ch. 18.   † 15 Car. II. ch. 7.

" Our annual remittances and debts to Great-
" Britain now encreafe with our diftreffes; our
" fubfcriptions for loans have been lately filled
" from Great-Britain; our eftates when fold, are
" purchafed by Englifhmen; our leafes, when
" they expire, are raifed by abfentees; the drain
" is become greater than all our means can fup-
" ply; ?our manufactures find little demand for
" their work; the farmers fell their produce with
" difficulty; our land rents, indeed, are eftimated at
" near three millions fterling, but our land-holders
" will foon be obliged to reduce them. We allow
" that feveral of your reftrictions upon us, have
" lately been much foftened, or modified, but the
" want of an annual profit in our intercourfe with
" Great Britain equal to our remittances ftill pre-
" vails, and is every hour more felt. By the un-
" fortunate fituation of the colonies, we have loft
" even our old refuge in emigrations. After hav-
" ing for many years taken Britifh manufactures,
" to the annual amount of *two millions* fterling, we
" are for the prefent reduced to *non-importation*
" agreements *, as a meafure, not of expediency,
" but

---

* It ought to have been anfwered, " We *(the Irifh)*
" fend more than that to England, with this difference,
" that the whole amount of ours, is the produce, or ma-
" nufacture of Ireland—the true fource of the wealth of a
" country; while the half of Englifh exports are of foreign
" produce—

"but of neceſſity. It would have ſuited the generoſity of our feelings, and the affection which we bear towards you, to have made our repreſentations in better and more peaceable times; but you ſee that our circumſtances are urgent, and that your recent indulgences are inſufficient. We deſire, therefore, A FREE TRADE, otherwiſe our diſtreſſes muſt, if poſſible, encreaſe, and the conveniency of our ports will continue of no more uſe to us, than a beautiful proſpect to a man ſhut up in a dungeon*."

Great-Britain loſes whenever Ireland is deprived of any reaſonable gain—and with reſpect to the ſituation of the latter for the weſtern navigation, we know that it is the intereſt of a dominion to carry on her commerce, from whatever corner ſhe can conduct it to the beſt advantage, and it would be thought a groſs abſurdity in the city of London, if, becauſe Briſtol is ſo ſituated as to have an advantage in the Iriſh trade, *the former ſhould deſire to have the port of the latter ſhut up.*

In all theſe reaſonings, the commercial and political intereſts, *are inſeparably blended.* When the liberty of commerce *is unequally enjoyed,* one part of an

---

" produce.—Non-importation would have raiſed in Ireland—we take more than 1,000,000l. of their linens, and they take 3,000,000l. of our woollens—the two ſtaples."

* Page 146.

an empire may be in danger of becoming a burden to the other. An increase of support in and of the common exertions, might, in course of time, result to Ireland from the advancement of her trade, and from the produce of duties, analogous to those of Great-Britain.

It is sometimes found, that a liberty to export manufactures, increases the produce of raw materials beyond the demand of the particular manufacture; and from the experience of the linen trade, it might be doubted whether less woollen yarn would be exported to Great-Britain by Ireland, if the export of manufactured woollens were less restrained; in which case, the smuggling of raw wool to the Continent of Europe might be checked*.

We are not, however, to proceed with that short-sighted wisdom, which may enable us to shun the mere difficulty of a day; nor to act upon the spur of a moment †.

The Irish, though at all times, she has had full liberty to manufacture goods for her own consumption, the consumers have hitherto found it easier to purchase from England, many articles, both of luxury and convenience, than to make them at home.

Amidst the difficulties which time, and the fostering attention of this country, alone can enable Ireland

---

* Page 160. † Page 163.

Ireland to overcome, it deserves remark, that she has little coal, is ill provided with wood, and is nearly without inland navigations. In short, the constitution and establishment of a flourishing empire, imply a well regulated order throughout the nation, a steady and effective police, habits f docility and industry, skill in manufactures, and large capitals in trade; all which can be the result only of a continued and gradual progress, aided by a combination of other favouring circumstances *.

Colonel FITZPATRICK†.

I am anxious that satisfaction should be given to the Irish nation, and that they should learn, that this country is well disposed *to give every necessary satisfaction*. This is particularly to be wished, because pains have been taken to spread ideas, that what has been done is not sufficient for the security of Ireland, and surmises have been thrown out against the friends of order and reason, *who were convinced of the rectitude of the intentions of Britain*.

Dec. 19, 1782.

Mr. FOX.

I take the first moment to declare, that the intentions of those Ministers who sent the repeal of the

---

* Page 166.

† Colonel Fitzpatrick begged leave to call the attention of Government to the circumstance, which had given some blame to the people of Ireland, *the decision of an Irish cause in the Court of King's Bench in England.*

the Declaratory Act, *were thereby to make a complete, absolute, and perpetual surrender of the British legislative and judicial supremacy over Ireland.* This *was the intention of Government* *; and it is clear to the conviction, both of Ministers and of the Gentlemen of Ireland, who interested themselves in the business, that the manner in which this is done, is the best possible way, and the least liable to exception. *Dec.* 19, 1782.

Lord BEAUCHAMP.

I have always understood it to be the privilege of a Member of Parliament, that when he has any particular business in the House, it was not to be taken out of his hands *by another* †. This is a privilege I would never resign; a friend to *both* kingdoms, my only object is to secure *a lasting harmony* between Great-Britain and Ireland; and if I should be able to root out every remains of jealousy, *my* great object will be accomplished, and I shall sit down *the happiest of men!*

E 2 *Dec.* 20, 1782.

* No one will surely dispute Mr. Fox's authority.

† This was occasioned by Mr. William Grenville giving notice, that he should move for a call of the House, *at an earlier day* than the 22d of January (the day on which Lord Beauchamp moved the Call) when a motion would be made relative to Ireland.

Mr.

Mr. EDEN.

A diſſatisfaction has ſomehow ſince ariſen, but I ſtill continue to think, that it ought not to have ariſen, for it ſhewed beyond a poſſible doubt *, not merely the good faith, but the induſtrious anxiety of England, *to gratify Ireland in the point of free legiſlation.*

I feel myſelf ever diſpoſed to think, and to ſpeak of Ireland with gratitude, with affection, and with reſpect; but I do not think her at this hour an object of fear to any nation under the Sun; ſhe neither has, nor will have her due importance in the great ſcale of the globe, till ſhe can be induced to think herſelf ſecure *in quitting politics, and purſuing commerce; it is my object and wiſh to forward for her that happy and important moment.*

Jan. 22, 1783.

Mr. FOX.

By the actual repeal of the 6 Geo. I. Great-Britain certainly, *and to all intents and purpoſes,* relinquiſhed *every ſhadow of juriſdiction, and ſupremacy.*

Jan. 22, 1783.

Mr. EDEN.

I relied on a treaty being opened † between the Parliaments of Great-Britain and Ireland, for the purpoſes

---

* Mr. Fox's propoſition on the 17th of May.
† Voted for the addreſs of the 17th of May laſt.

purposes of arranging not only the points already specified, but all the great questions involved in the future events of peace and war, foreign alliances, commercial treaties, limitation of armies, building and support of navies. proportionable supplies, *with the whole immense detail under each of these heads.* I shall then, *and not till then*, think that the connection is established; and when the two kingdoms have thus realized and secured one constitution, one commerce, one King, one friend, one enemy, and one fate, it will become impossible for any man, *to wish the prosperity of the one country more ardently, or more earnestly, than the prosperity of the other.*   *Jan.* 22, 1783.

HOUSE OF LORDS.

Earl of HILSBOROUGH.

I WAS called by my Sovereign, from a private situation, to assist in his councils. I had formed my opinion, as an object of leading consequence, respecting the state of Ireland. I imparted my thoughts, my motives, and intended conduct, to those with whom I am to act; *and upon the idea of a full confirmation, and support of the Crown and its servants, I consented to come into office.*

I wish not to be understood, as dictating any measures, or pledging myself for the result; what I mean is merely this, that such and such were my opinions; that they were approved of, and that I would wait with anxious suspence, and chearfully abide the event, and in common with the rest of his Majesty's subjects, submit to the sense of Parliament; but if, on the other hand, as suggested as a general charge against Government, that the conditions on which I came into place, should be violated, or departed from, or that a perfect good faith should not be preserved, the same motives which induced me to accept of the seals, a view to serve my country, *to cause relief to be given to Ireland.*

Ireland, and advance the interest and prosperity of every part of the British Empire, would point out to me the propriety of retiring again into a private station; *when the end for which I left it*, shall be found no longer attainable, or in other words, when it will not be in my power to serve my country.* Nov. 25, 1779 †.

Earl

* To procure, in conjunction with the rest of the Ministers of the Crown, such relief for Ireland, as she might be entitled to expect from Great-Britain.

† On the 11th May, 1779, the *late Marquis of Rockingham* moved an immediate consideration of the distressed, and impoverished state of the kingdom of Ireland, and such effectual measures as should promote *the common strength, wealth, and commerce of his Majesty's subjects in Great-Britain and Ireland.*—After describing the *private* as well as *public* distresses of Ireland, in the most feeling language, the noble Marquis proceeded to contrast the deserts of the Irish nation, whose loyalty kept pace with the extent and magnitude of the calamities they felt. He instanced, in particular, their friendly and affectionate behaviour since the commencement of the American war; the zeal and fidelity of that kingdom, in the time of the two last Scotch rebellions; the uncommon efforts she made during the late war, and her uniform loyalty, and attachment, to this country, in every trying exigency, when engaged in a foreign war.

He said, he hoped, the importance of the object would strike every noble Lord with the propriety, nay, the absolute necessity of his motion, that the House would treat it *with that temper, coolness, and moderation* which it so apparently

parently merited, and attend to it as a matter, in which every man in the nation was moft deeply interefted. He trufted, that their Lordfhips would not be led away *by any partial ideas or narrow diftinctions of local benefit or advantage**, but meet it fairly as a queftion of State, in which both kingdoms had an equal intereft. He would be extremely forry, that this, or that town, or diftrict, *that Manchefter, or Glafgow, or any other place, would fupercede or render of non-effect the wifdom of their Lordfhips' deliberations.* He wifhed farther, that on the prefent occafion, *all party or perfonal confiderations would give way to the general good* †, and that as they all meant *the fame thing*, the interefts of both kingdoms, their Lordfhips' would not entertain a fecound opinion on the fubject. It was a great object, and fhould neither be loft, abandoned, or evaded; it had for fome years been unfortunately too much neglected, but matters were at length arrived juft at that critical ftate, which would render it not only unwife and impolitic to lofe a moment, but would afford an inftance of obftinacy and want of feeling, *little fhort of political infanity.*

* The noble Marquis appears to be well aware *of the partial ideas, and narrow diftinctions, of local benefit, or advantage,* that would probably *be ftirred up againft* the adjufting fuch a commercial intercourfe, as might be thought for the *reciprocal* benefit of both countries; and no doubt, the Houfe of Lords will be fufficiently guarded againft any thing of the kind, on the prefent occafion.

† It is to be hoped that Mr. Fox, and his friends, will bear in mind the falutary advice and wholefome admonition of the noble Marquis, whofe virtues they fo juftly revered, and whofe memory they hold fo dear, and not fuffer the real intereft of Great-Britain and Ireland to give way *to party or perfonal confiderations.*

F

Earl of HILSBOROUGH.

Previous to my acceptance of the seals, as Secretary of State, I desired to know the intention of his Majesty's Ministers *(Lord North, &c.)* and the opinion of his Council, relative to future measures, respecting Ireland; and received every assurance from them, that Government was thoroughly disposed to co-operate with Parliament, in giving to that kingdom, *such an extension of trade as would put her on a footing with Great-Britain on the scale of commerce* *. Dec. 1, 1779 †.

---

* As the *memory* of Lord North, and his friends, are so apt to fail them, it is rather a *lucky* circumstance for them, that it can be refreshed by so respectable an authority.

† The late Marquis of Rockingham was so very sensible of the necessity there was for doing something for effectually relieving the distresses of Ireland, and had the object so much at heart, that in the course of the debate on the 11th May, 1779, he repeated with some warmth, that Ireland had been cruelly and injuriously treated, and that it would present a mixture of folly and ingratitude, which nothing but the dullest obstinacy and ignorance could explain, if we refuse to lighten *those intolerable burthens* which the restriction *of our trade laws* laid upon that *loyal, affectionate, and enduring people.* The *Duke of Beaufort*, though he possessed a considerable property in Ireland, said he should chearfully assist in any measure, for giving the Irish that species of relief which their situation demanded. *Lord Townshend*, in expressions of the warmest affections for the people of Ireland, pleaded their distresses first in very forcible language; and said, he should

Earl GOWER.

I had the good fortune to unite the House last Session, upon the terms of the Address to the Throne*. I was in hopes that something *effectual* for

be wanting in the feelings which gratitude ought ever to inspire, if he did not take the present opportunity of testifying his regard for them, and his earnestness to procure them every degree of redress and indulgence, which their melancholy situation demanded, which justice dictated, and generosity and national gratitude rendered a positive duty on the part of a great nation. He should, in point of union and national strength, *ever consider England and Ireland as one country, and the people of each equally bound and connected by the same object, the prosperity of the whole.* The Duke of Richmond also in a very able speech, endeavoured to show, that all local distinctions were the creatures of prejudice and selfishness. He said, that Ireland and England *were in fact the same nation and people*; that any distinction made in favour of the *latter*, was a piece of injustice to the *former*. A great, loyal, and a brave people, were not to be ruined, beggared, or oppressed, because Manchester thought *this*, or *this*, or *that country* were alarmed. All these petty motives must cease to operate, nor be permitted to influence our public Councils, which ought never to lose sight of justice and sound policy. He was for an union; but not an union of Legislature, *but an union of hearts, hands, of affections,* and *interests*.

* The Address was as follows.—" That this House
" take into consideration the distressed and impoverished
" state

for the relief of Ireland would have arisen *from the unanimous concurrence of their Lordships* in the amendment I then had the honour to propose †. If, however, nothing has been done, for the relief of that

"state of the kingdom of Ireland, and being of opinion,
"that it is confonant to justice and true policy to remove
"the causes of discontent by a redress of grievances, and,
"in order to demonstrate the sense which the House en-
"tertains of the merits of that loyal and well deserving
"nation, this House doth think it highly expedient, that
"this important business should be no longer neglected,
"and that an humble Address be presented to his Majesty,
"That his Majesty would be graciously pleased to take the
"matter into his most serious consideration, and direct his
"Minister to prepare, and lay before Parliament such par-
"ticulars relative to the trade and manufactures of Ireland,
"as may enable the national wisdom to pursue effectual
"measures for promoting the common strength, wealth,
"and commerce, of his Majesty's subjects in both king-
"doms."

† The following is the *amended* address which was carried *nem. con.* "That an humble address be presented to
"his Majesty, that he will be pleased to take into his
"gracious consideration, the distressed and impoverished
"state of the loyal and well-deserving people of Ireland,
"and to direct an account to be laid before Parliament of
"such particulars relative to the trade and manufactures of
"Ireland, as may enable the national wisdom to pursue
"methods for promoting the common strength, wealth
"and commerce, of his Majesty's subjects in both king-
"doms."

that country, which I am pretty sure is the case, I assure the House, that I have done every thing in my power to keep my word, which I formerly pledged to the House, and am ready to acknowledge, but I must add, in my own justification, that my efforts have proved totally unfruitful.

May 11, 1779 *.

Earl of CARLISLE.

I rise to express my entire approbation of the motions †, and to bear my testimony to the zeal and loyalty

---

* His Lordship added, that he had, for some years, presided at the Council Table, and had seen such things pass there, that no man of honour and conscience, could any longer sit there. The situation of Great Britain and Ireland required *sincerity and activity of Council*. There is no doubt as to the cause of the noble Earl's disgust.— The ministers (*Lord North*, &c.) had certainly pledged themselves to do something *effectual for the Relief of Ireland*, and none was given.

† " First, That it is the opinion of this House, that
" the Act of 6th Geo. I. intituled, An Act for the better
" securing the dependency of Ireland upon the Crown of
" Great Britain, ought to be repealed. Second, That
" it is the opinion of this House, That it is indispensible
" to the interest and happiness of both countries, that the
" connection between them should be established by mu-
" tual consent, upon a solid and permanent footing, and
" that an humble address be presented to his Majesty, that
" his Majesty will be graciously pleased, to take such mea-
" sures

loyalty of the Irish, particularly of the honourable conduct of the Volunteers, and the liberal offers made of their service, when Ireland was threatened with an attack. Had I been more persuaded than I am, that Ireland had ever relinquished its right of free legislation, which I know they neither have nor can give up, I should still have thought it wise to accede to their claim; because I know, that from the gratitude and affection of the country, and the wisdom of Parliament, much more advantage would arise to Great Britain, than by maintaining any offensive and ill-founded pretensions to a controul over them.

May 17, 1782.

Earl of HILSBOROUGH.

I hope, and believe, ministers are sincere in their good intentions towards Ireland. I am persuaded, they have no other object with regard to this country, and to that, but to promote the interest of both; but persons at a distance, *who are not so well convinced of their good intentions towards*

" sures as his Majesty in his Royal wisdom shall think most
" conducive to that important end. " Both motions were agreed to without a division. Both the Resolutions were moved by the Earl of Shelburne, and supported by the Earl of Carlisle, Lord Camden, Duke of Leinster, Duke of Chandos, and Duke of Richmond.

wards Ireland *, may conftrue every little delay into matter of fufpicion and alarm; and, therefore, I conceive, *I beft fhow myfelf the friend of government, by cautioning them of their danger.* June 3, 1783.

Duke of PORTLAND.

I always have been, and always fhall be ready, to do every thing in my power to cement the connection between Great-Britain and Ireland, on terms of mutual affection and mutual intereft.

April 24, 1783. †

---

* It is now three years fince the noble Lord was promifed by *Lord North, &c.* that relief fhould be given to Ireland, and though none has ever been rendered, yet the noble Lord has ftill fo much faith in their affurances, *as to believe them fincere in their intentions towards Ireland,* nay, for his Lordfhip's part, *he is perfuaded of it,* whatever perfons may think, *who are at a diftance,* and may conftrue every little delay *into matter of fufpicion and alarm.* —What will the noble Lord think then, fhould this fame *Lord North* be found to oppofe the commercial intercourfe now eftablifhing between Great-Britain and Ireland?

† On the fecond reading of the Irifh Judicature Bill.

*** The public are refpectfully informed, that the fpeeches that fhall be delivered by the Oppofition, in the Lords and Commons, on Irifh Affairs, will be faithfully *contrafted* with thofe of the prefent publication.

APPENDIX.

APPENDIX.

THE COMMERCIAL RESOLUTIONS OF THE IRISH PARLIAMENT, IN THEIR PRESENT SESSION, VINDICATED.

To which is added,

AN AUTHENTIC COPY OF THE RESOLUTIONS.

Abstract of a Letter from a Member of the British House of Commons, written soon after the late General Election to a Member of the Irish House.

SIR,

May, 1784.

WHEN Ireland was dependent on Great Britain, it was wished by several friends of both Countries to render dependence beneficial to her. Two bills were therefore brought into the British Parliament, one allowing to Ireland freedom of Exportation to our Colonies and Settlements, the other a like Freedom of Importation from

from thence, both denied to all Foreign Independent countries.

These were meant as experiments, upon a narrow scale, which, if found advantageous to Ireland without prejudicing Britain, might and ought to be extended further; were it for no other purpose than to preserve Irish dependence by the surest and only justifiable means.

The first Bill passed, but absurdly mutilated; and the little that remained of it was rendered useless by a still more absurd suppression of the second Bill, as an export-trade cannot subsist where imports are prohibited,

When Ireland became independent, with an unrestrained freedom of trade to all countries except Great Britain, I wished her friendship should be preserved by opening the Ports of Great Britain upon the same terms that open those of Ireland to Her, convinced as I then was and still am that the comparative magnitude of British Capitals, lowness of interest and superiority of skill, with all their necessary consequences, would, under an equality of duties, secure a continuance of the same advantages to Great Britain which she before invidiously possessed under an inequality which operated as a total Prohibition on her side of almost all manufactures except Linen, while she was treated in Ireland, *literally*, as the most favoured Nation in the scale of duties.

I am aware of the objection, that when Ireland becomes rich, those advantages will lessen with her increase and at length totally cease. But wealth, earned and employed in trade, will ever in a progressive state maintain at least the superiority it had gained: improvements of old manufactures and discoveries of new will more frequently appear, as they now do at Manchester, Birmingham, &c. &c. and Dublin growing *richer* in her progressive state, but advancing by slower paces, will become a better customer than *poor* Dublin ever was

But, be this as it may, independent Ireland will never be satisfied under the present inequality of duties. It is a badge of slavery which she never will patiently bear, and British Parliament alone has the means of removing it, by lowering the duties there to the Irish standard. The attempt now meditating in Ireland to increase them there in the article of woollens, supported by the most false assertions

tions and most absurd arguments, would, if it could succeed, certainly be fatal to Ireland, as it would soon be retaliated by England on linens and other articles, while multiplied restraints would at length end in a total prohibition of trade in both countries, such as is only known in a state of war; yet England even now is the best customer Ireland has, giving a longer credit than any other country can for what she sends, and paying quicker remittances for what she receives: Two returns in a year upon the same capital, which double its profits, make one thousand pounds virtually as much as two, where returns are made but once in the same space of time.

You have here the thoughts of an old infirm man, who has bid farewell to all politicks, English and Irish: and who, though elected into this Parliament, is determined to vacate his seat; yet, if you think as I do upon this subject, and believe that the expedient will satisfy Ireland, I will defer the execution of my unalterable purpose, until I shall have had an early opportunity of throwing myself and my opinions upon the House of Commons, as I have often done without hazard to the popularity of Ministers, with whom I was connected, if my opinion were not relished; and willing to give them all the merit if they were approved. In this spirit I now write to you and have the honour to be, &c. &c.

Purport of the Answer received to the above Letter.

"NOTHING but protecting duties, heavier upon Merchandise imported from Great Britain than upon Irish Merchandise imported there, will satisfy Ireland."

WHILE a system of duties seemed to be thus insisted upon by Ireland, not equalized by the value of similar articles in commerce, as is the universal rule of Tariffs between all Independent States: while in that system allowances were claimed for the inferior abilities of Ireland to supply Great Britain to purchase from her the same articles at the same rates, impossible to be proportioned so as to form a fair standard of Trade; and while these arbitrary conditions were to be imposed by threats and violence proceeding to overt act: of cruel Barbarism, no friend of both countries would insult Great Britain by offering propositions to her Parliament which if accepted there, would be reprobated and spurned by the Irish Parliament, the whole Nation applauding their conduct.

Thus circumstanced I retired in despair, and if the Ministers of Great Britain had then introduced any accommodating propositions here, in the first instance, they, instead of asserting the dignity of their country by insisting upon that precedence, would have tarnished and debased it: Those who are in the wrong should first make concessions; or if, as happily was the fact in Ireland, faction, ignorance and frenzy, did not speak the sentiments of the people, it behoved the honour and fidelity of their representatives to declare the difference, by offering a plan to the sister Kingdom supported, and only supported by Equality, Justice and mutual Interest.

But if, having thus acted, the British Parliament should again be influenced, as it was in the two Bills already mentioned, by the mistaken interest of narrow minded men against one common universal interest the Irish Parliament, though without a prospect of Ireland ever becoming the Emporium of trade, as was hyperbolically expressed in a late debate, would be the unrivall'd possessor of firmness, liberality, reason and justice.

Vilius argentum est auro, vertutibus aurum.

That an opposition here to the Resolutions of the Irish Parliament proceeds from false conceptions, we shall now endeavour to prove by stating those objections which have reached our knowledge; and giving the answers which have occured to us.

Objection 1st. If Ireland be permitted to export Sugars to Great Britain, she will smuggle in for that purpose Foreign Sugars purchased at a lower price; and by these means undersel British Sugars at their own home market.

Answer. The Revenue of Ireland would then suffer doubly, first by being defrauded of the duty payable upon
imported

imported Muscavado Sugars, and again by paying upon their exportation a drawback of duties never received, or a premium when refined, more than an equivalent for those duties. The Parliament and Government of Ireland will therefore be most importantly interested in preventing that practice.

Secondly, the Irish consumption of Sugars is considerable, and is chiefly, if not intirely, of Sugars brought from Great Britain. Why then is not that consumption now entirely supplied with smuggled Sugars? these would find a demand to a considerable amount, although the British Ports were, as they still are, shut to Irish exportation.

Objection 2d. French, Dutch, Danish, &c. Sugars, will be entered as our Plantation Sugars, and, though they pay the same duties, they will be bought cheaper, and so circumstanced will be exported to Britain entitled to a drawback there of the duties paid, or to a premium, as the case shall happen upon re-exportation.

Answer. The Irish Revenue will be no gainer by this traffick, and therefore the government will have no interest in conniving at it. Nor is the difference of price such as to tempt the fraudulent Merchant to encounter the risk of being discovered.

Objection 3d. Irish Merchants would be the sole importers of Sugars into Ireland directly from the British Plantations.

Answer. This objection is the reverse of the foregoing, but the second answer is applicable to it: The Irish are at liberty now to import Sugars directly, to the full amount of Irish consumption, yet small have been the quantities so imported, since the freedom of a direct importation has been allowed to Ireland.

Objection 4th. British Merchants will transport themselves and their capitals into Ireland.

Answer. Why is not this supposition verified by some instances now to be produced? They certainly will not send their capitals, and stay themselves behind, trusting to the management of others. But inconvenient and disagreeable as this removal would be to themselves and their families, they would find it more difficult to procure sugar-bakers to remove, and persuade all the subordinate manufactures to accompany them. Yet should this be
effected

effected, they cannot transport their sugar-houses, nor the materials of which they are built. They must be sold here at the price of rubbish; for the buildings cannot be converted to new uses; and the same is true of the utensils. All these must again be provided in Ireland, when the adventurers arrive there, where it will be found, that coals, and many other articles necessary to the refining of sugars, are dearer than in England.

But these are far from being all the disadvantages to be encountered in Ireland: a credit of three years, usually given to the planter by the merchant his creditor, must still be continued, while the sugar baker and refiner will require from the merchant a longer respite of payment than is allowed in England, where the shop-keeper, their customer, is sooner and more punctually paid by the customer. Quick returns of small profits, the life of trade, are only to be found in wealthy countries; and men so enriched, will hardly emigrate into poor countries, to meet with delay and disappointments, not to be compensated by cheapness of manual labour, or commodiousness of situation.

But though mere manual labour, such as is employed in delving and ditching, which require no skill, may be hired cheaper from a wretch in poverty and rags, it is much dearer and less valuable in every work of art, shortened in numberless instances by engines enabling one man to do more than many. A few years since, there was not a single crane on the Quay of Cork.

The history of commerce rarely produces an instance of a wealthy trader going into a poor country to increase his wealth: but if cheapness of manual labour necessarily invited large capitals, no poor country would long continue poor; nor indeed any rich country long continue rich, mutually changing and rechanging conditions, as the price of such labour sunk or rose. But though poverty emigrates, or starves, wealth remains fixt to that soil where it grew; and flourishes in proportion as it spreads its roots

deeper

deeper and wider there. Transplant an oak and it perishes *.

What has been said of cheap labour, is equally true of commodious situation. The richest mercantile towns in England have the worst harbours: Milford scarcely contains a vessel in its excellent haven, except passing to or from some other port, while the dry mud of Bristol is crouded with ships detained there by many contrary winds, and exposed to fire from the houses but a few yards distant, after having made their way through a most perilous channel to the merchant's warehouses. Were those merchants asked, why they do not remove to Milford Haven? and were the same question proposed to sugar-bakers, glass-men, copper manufacturers, &c. &c. &c. their answer would be, a smile of contempt. Yet predictions much more impossible of emigrations to Dublin, Cork, Waterford, and Limerick, are gravely made, and anxiously listened to.

But if all we have said were false, and Cork were to rival Bristol, while London would be rivalled by Dublin in West Indian imports, though the British merchant would then have a just cause for sorrow and opposition, the West India planters should rejoice in a view of two markets instead of being confined to one.

This leads us to another objection.

Objection 5th. The Planter indebted to his factor in Britain, as most Planters confessedly are, would change hands and defraud his creditor by consignments into Ireland.

Answer. This expedient though troublesome and expensive to the Creditor, would not leave him without a remedy, as the Planter's property in the West Indies would be subject to his demand. It is reported that one or two attempts of this nature were made in England, but defeated.

---

* England undersels Ireland at her own Markets with Cloth made of Irish Woollen Yarn, for which a duty is paid in Ireland upon exportation; and the difference of price is greater in proportion to the fineness of the Fabrick,

Nor

Nor has it, I believe, been heard that such base policy was, in any instance, practised in supplying the consumption of Ireland ever since a direct importation has been allowed there.

The Planters therefore need not be solicitous to refute so undeserved a calumny, by uniting with the British Merchants. Nor is such solicitude the real cause of an union clearly accounted for without admitting an infamous imputation upon any number of worthy, but generous men : most Planters are indebted to their Factors, and by consequence are under their power and influence.

There are however many planters in opulent circumstances, free from all restraint, who, though the advertising merchants would blend them in one general description, will, no doubt, separate and distinguish themselves from their enthralled bretheren.

But, if what we have advanced upon this subject be well founded, the merchant requires no sacrifice from the planters of their interest to his; his fears are as vain as those of a North British member of Parliament were, when he foretold in a speech against the importation of Irish live cattle into Britain, that, if it was permitted, an Ox would be as rare an animal in our fields as a Lion.

Objection 6*th*. When the ports of Great Britain shall be always open to the importation of grain and flour from Ireland, let the price be ever so low; immense quantities will be poured in from thence, detrimental to the British landlord and tenant.

Answer. ' The dry climate of South Britain is universally more favourable to harvests, than that of rainy Ireland, and the same true of most parts of North Britain. Potatoes are therefore the general food of Ireland. Yet a great proportion of the comparatively small quantity of grain and flour, consumed there, was supplied by England, until a bounty was granted in Ireland upon exportation ; and we believe that the balance, though not so great, is still in favour of England.

Should there be, in an unusual change of seasons, a scarcity here when there is an abundance in Ireland, a supply from thence will be more to our advantage, than from any other country, and Irish cheapness will then be a common blessing to the sister kingdoms.

But

APPENDIX X.

But should there be a superfluity in both, Britain will preferably consume her own grain and flour free from freight and hazard, which she must pay for; nor will Ireland send her produce to an over-stocked market, while the World is open to her.

It is true that Scotland, in particular, is supplied with Irish oats and meal, in great quantities for her own consumption. But it is also true that Scotch Merchants, and others in parts of South Britain, purchase more than is wanted for that purpose, immediately after harvest, when the miserable Irish tenant is obliged to thresh out his corn, for payment of rent in November to a distressed and relentless landlord. From hence it often happens that Irish corn is exported at a much lower price, sometimes scarcely exceeding one half of what it afterwards bears, when brought back to drained and starving Ireland.

But admitting that North Britain, chiefly concerned in this question, should sometimes so abound with oats of her own growth, as to render a prohibition of importation advantageous, which seldom happens even for a short time, she will at all other times be a gainer, by cheapness in Ireland.

Having vindicated, we hope, sufficiently the Resolutions of the Irish Parliament, we shall now take notice of an *objection* made by some of its members *to the 10th Article*, charged with granting a *tribute* annually payable to Britain, as if a small contribution to the support of a Maritime Force, necessary to the common protection of both countries, deserved a degrading appellation; more especially as the application of that supply to any specifick naval service, is to be solely directed by the Irish Parliament, although it is to arise out of an hereditary revenue, settled more than a century past by an Irish Parliament upon the King of England and Ireland.

The eventual supply, for such it only is, now to be granted, will depend for its existence and quantity upon an increase of Irish trade, necessarily requiring a larger establishment of force and expence. If there be no increase, there will be no supply, and if there be an increase, the supply will rise only in proportion to it.

APPENDIX.

When assistance has been purchased by Great Britain, as it has been almost in every war, from allies unconnected with her by any common interest, and without any of the qualifying circumstances, which attend what those, whom we have alluded to, call a tribute, however those subsidised powers may have been blamed for submitting to such terms, Great Britain has been often served but never dishonoured by becoming thus tributary to many a petty Prince. Yet in this sense only would Ireland be tributary to Great Britain, for her assistance by paying an annual sum, more properly termed a subsidy, than a tribute.

Should the adjustment now proposed by the Parliament of Ireland be rejected here, God grant that without any degree of prescience exceeding what is derived from experience and a slight knowledge of History, we shall not be better warranted than the abovementioned North British Member was in his prediction, when we foretel that the King of Great Britain and Ireland, while he retains both chraracters, giving his assent to the bills of each Parliament, will not be able to exercise that function of Royal legislative power consistently with the duty of a common Father to all his subjects.

We shall therefore conclude by hoping that whatever opposition may be consistently given by those who either voted against the two bills mentioned in the foregoing abstract, or did not vote at all, none who joined in their support upon the principle that Great Britain and Ireland should retain all their respective natural or acquired advantages, but subject to the same duties upon importation and upon exportation to Foreign Markets, will oppose a further enlargement of the trade of Ireland grounded upon the same principles, certain as it is that the acquired advantages of Great Britain incomparably exceed the superiority of those natural to Ireland. Nay we are far from conceding any superiority to Ireland in the sum total of gifts gratuitously bestowed by Providence without Labour and Industry.

Resolutions

Resolutions of the House of Commons of Ireland.

Resolved I. That it is the opinion of this committee, that it is highly important to the interest of the British Empire, that the trade between Great Britain and Ireland be extended as much as possible, and for that purpose, that the intercourse and commerce be finally settled and regulated on permanent and equitable principles, for the mutual benefit of both countries.

Resolved II. That towards carrying into full effect so desirable a settlement, it is fit and proper that all articles, not the growth of Great Britain and Ireland, should be imported into each Kingdom from the other, under the same regulations, and at the same duties, if subject to duties, to which they are liable when imported directly from the place of their growth, product, or manufacture; and that all duties originally paid on importation, to either country respectively, shall be drawn back on exportation to the other.

Resolved III. That for the same purpose, that it is proper that no prohibition should exist in either country against the importation, use, or sale of any article, the growth, product, or manufacture of the other; and that the duty on the importation of every such article, if subject to duty in either country, should be precisely the same in one country as in the other, except where an addition may be necessary in either country, in consequence of an internal duty on any such article of its own consumption.

Resolved IV. That in all cases where the duties on articles of the growth, product, or manufacture of either country are different on the importation into the other, it would be expedient that they should be reduced in the Kingdom where they are the highest, to the amount payable in the other, and that all such articles should be exportable from the Kingdom into which they shall be imported, as free from duty as the similar commodities or home manufactures of the same Kingdom.

Resolved V. That for the same purpose, it is also proper that in all cases where either Kingdom shall charge articles of its own consumption with an internal duty on the manufacture, or a duty on the material, the same manufacture, when imported from the other, may be charged with a further duty on importation, to the same amount as the internal duty on the manufacture, or to an amount adequate to countervail the duty on the material, and shall be entitled to such drawbacks or bounties on exportation, as may leave the same subject to no heavier burthen than the home-made manufacture; such further duty to continue so long only as the internal consumption shall be charged with the duty or duties; to balance which it shall be imposed, or until the manufacture coming from the other Kingdom shall be subjected

there

there to an equal burthen, not drawn back or compensated on exportation.

Resolved VI. That in order to give permanency to the settlements now intended to be established, it is necessary that no prohibition, or new or additional duties, should be hereafter imposed in either kingdom, on the importation of any article of the growth, product, or manufacture of the other, except, such additional duties, as may be requisite to balance duties on internal consumption, pursuant to the foregoing resolution.

Resolved VII. That for the same purpose, it is necessary further, that no prohibitions, or new additional duties, should be hereafter imposed on either kingdoms, on the exportation of any article of native growth, product, or manufacture, from thence to the other, except such as either kingdom may deem expedient from time to time, upon corn, meal, malt, flour, and biscuit; and also, except where there now exists any prohibition, which is not reciprocal, or any duty, which is not equal, in both kingdoms; in every which case the prohibition may be made reciprocal, or the duties raised so as to make them equal.

Resolved VIII. That for the same purpose, it is necessary that no bounties whatsoever should be paid, or payable in either kingdom, on the exportation of any article to the other, except such as relate to corn, meal, malt flour, and biscuits, and such as are in the nature of drawbacks or compensations for duties paid; and that no bounties should be granted in this kingdom, on the exportation of any article imported from the British Plantations, or any manufacture made of such article, unless in cases where a similar bounty is payable in Britain on exportation from thence or where such bounty is merely in the nature of a drawback, or compensation of or for duties paid over and above any duties paid thereon in Britain.

Resolved IX. That it is expedient for the general benefit of the British Empire, that the importation of articles from foreign States should be regulated from time to time, in each kingdom, on such terms as may afford an effectual preference to the importation of similar articles of the growth, produce, or manufacture of the other.

Resolved X. That for the better protection of trade, whatever sum the gross hereditary revenue of this kingdom (after deducting all drawbacks, repayments, or bounties granted in the nature of drawbacks) shall produce annually, over and above the sum of £.   should be appropriated towards the support of the *Naval Force* of the Empire, in *such manner as the Parliament of this Kingdom* shall direct.

A SHORT,

APPENDIX.

A SHORT VIEW

OF THE

PROPOSALS

LATELY MADE FOR THE

Final Adjuſtment of the Commercial Syſtem between GREAT-BRITAIN and IRELAND.

THE Propoſals from Ireland, for ſettling the Trade between this Country and that, upon principles of equity and mutual benefit; and above all, for uniting more cloſely the two kingdoms, are undoubtedly of the greateſt national importance. With this view, it is material to examine, whether the objections raiſed, outweigh the manifeſt advantage of ſuch a ſettlement.

It is intended therefore, to ſtate briefly a few facts, in order to ſhew what Ireland enjoys already, from former conceſſions, ſo as to be able to appretiate juſtly what is now propoſed to be given; for the important purpoſes beofre ſtated.

It was the act of the 15th of Charles II. ch. 7, which for the firſt time confined to England alone, the liberty of ſending European produce to the Colonies, with a reſervation to Ireland to ſend ſervants, horſes, and victual; ſome few other articles have been allowed to be ſent from thence by ſubſequent ſtatutes.

It was the 22 and 23 Charles II. ch. 26, which firſt prohibited Tobacco, Sugar, Cotton, Dyeing Woods, and other enumerated produce of the Britiſh Colonies, from being ſent to Ireland, except through England: But theſe Acts were explained and enforced by ſubſequent Acts of Parliament: So that in Law and in Fact, none of the enumerated produce of the Britiſh

Plantations

Plantations before mentioned could be brought to Ireland in any other manner except through England, from that early period, to the year 1780.

It was at this time when the Irish Parliament had asked specifically for a free trade, as a redress of their grievances, that Lord North proposed and carried through the Act of 20 George III. chap. 10. this law completely opened the direct Trade between Ireland and the British Plantations in America and Africa: For it enacted, That any goods which may be legally imported from British America and Africa into Britain, may, in like manner, be directly imported from the said Plantations into Ireland; that goods may in the same direct manner be sent from Ireland to the said Colonies and Settlements; on condition however of paying the same duties in Ireland as shall be paid in Britain, and allowing the same draw-back. The Levant Trade was opened to Ireland during the same Session, by the 20 Geo. III. ch. 18.

When, in superaddition to these extensive grants, Mr. Fox proposed and carried through the Act of 22 George III. ch. 53, for admitting the Independence of the Irish Legislature, Ireland was left at its own discretion, to regulate its Commerce to all Foreign Countries; and every British Act of Parliament with regard to Commerce or the Customs ceased to be of any authority in Ireland. Lord North's Act delivered over to the Irish all the advantages of the Colony Trade:—Mr. Fox's Act gave to Ireland the Independent direction of its Commerce with Foreigners. By the first measure, the Irish were allowed to import directly all the Articles of West India Produce. By the second the Irish were enabled to send them, as they pleased, to all the Markets in Europe. It is not intended to dispute the propriety of these first concessions, though perhaps the mode of them might well be questioned; but whatever disadvantages have resulted, or may result, from either, or both of them, ought at least to be traced up to their original sources.

While the Irish Trade was in this manner made free to the Levant and to Europe, Africa, and America; that with Great Britain continued fettered by various restrictions; and in consequence, there subsisted a thousand fand embarrassments in the Commerce between the Sister-kingdoms, which ought on the contrary to be cherished as a Coast Trade. It is to be remembered too, that when the important concessions before enumerated were made by those Ministers, nothing was required, at least nothing was stipulated in return. No measure was then adopted for giving effect to the Act of Navigation, so delivered over (to use Mr. Fox's *present language*) to the custody of the Irish Custom-house Officers; and yet these same men, with a happy consistency for which they are so famous, now urge this as a charge against the System at present proposed.

Nothing was, however, done by either of them, towards examining into the state of the Manufactories of the two countries, with a view of removing the present, or guarding against future difficulties, and putting them on a footing of reciprocal advantages, so as to give a spur to the industry and exertions of each.

The war of drawbacks and bounties, the claims of equalizing and protecting duties, the agreements for non-importation and non-consumption of British Manufactures, and a general spirit of jealousy and discontent, were the natural consequences of these omissions.

In this distracted state were the affairs of Ireland delivered over to the present Ministers. In consequence of their investigations, proposals are now made to Parliament for a final settlement between the two kingdoms, which may be collected under three heads: 1st, That the produce of each kingdom shall be imported into the other upon equal duties, taking for that purpose the lowest rate of duty in each. 2dly, That Foreign Goods which had been imported into either, may be carried to the other, upon the same duties as if coming directly from the place of their growth: And, 3dly, That besides supporting the Civil and Military Establishment of Ireland, means shall be concerted for providing a Revenue applicable to the more general purposes of the Empire.

To the first measure what reasonable man can object, who considers the situation of both kingdoms, as to their religion and laws, their credit and capital, their industry and ingenuity; and who adverts to the fact, that British

Manufactures

Manufactures have for years succesfully carried on a competition with the Irish in their own Market, though they went thither loaded with taxes and charges of importation and sale?

If, however, any man entertains a doubt on this subject, let him suspend his opinion till the Evidence is produced which was promised by the Minister in the House of Commons, and stated to be the result of an accurate investigation of every Manufacture which can be affected by the arrangement; and let him in the mean time recollect, that the Irish Manufactures will come into this country burthened with duties, in general amounting to 10l. per cent. which is surely a sufficient protection for established Manufactures against any competition.

To the second measure some objections have indeed been made, chiefly with a view to the West-India Trade. It is suggested, that French Sugars will be smuggled from the West-Indies to Ireland, and from thence to Britain. It is said, as before mentioned, that the custody of the Act of Navigation is delivered to Ireland: And it is moreover asserted, that a breach would be made in that great bulwark of our maritime strength.

As to the first objection, it is surely apparent, that as the Law now stands upon Lord North's concession, Sugars may be equally smuggled from the West Indies to Ireland, and may be thence smuggled to Britain, with almost equal ease as if they were admitted to a lawful entry from Ireland to England.

Against this illicit Trade we have a double security; the invariable policy of France, confirmed by innumerable Edicts, has been to prevent all foreign ships from taking on board Sugars, &c. in their Colonies; and our Laws, both in England and Ireland, positively prohibit the importation of such produce from any parts, except from our own Colonies. It should be considered also, that Sugar, from its bulky passage, cannot easily be shipped or landed fraudently; and that, from its perishable nature, it is liable to sustain great loss in removal; it cannot be put on shore in open bays which smugglers frequent with other articles, but must be landed in some port.

Can the Irish smuggler enter into competition with the American smuggler for the same article? Can the Irish smuggler carry with *him* a sufficient equivalent in credit or goods, to buy a cargo of Sugar, considering how much the French Sugars have risen in price since the Peace? But, lastly, would the smuggler find an adequate advantage for his risques and his voyage, considering the small duty on Sugar, in comparison with its value, and considering the competition he would meet with from the Sugars lawfully imported?

As to the second objection, it may be allowed, that as far as the Act of Navigation is to operate as a law of Ireland, the execution of it must be entrusted to the Irish Revenue Officers: To their custody it was delivered by Lord North and Mr. Fox in 1780 and 1782; and there seems no valid reason for supposing, that the Irish Officers are less worthy of trust than the Custom-house Officers in the Colonies, or even in England. There is the same gradation of offices in the one kingdom as in the other, from the Comissioners of the Revenue to the Tidewaiter, who are all equally bound to execute their trust, and who may be all removed, if any misconduct shall be found.

That opening and extending still more the Navigation between the ports of the Sister Kingdoms, would destroy or enfeeble the principle of the Navigation Act, is an objection which surely requires some proof or explanation. The great purpose of that justly celebrated Law is, to raise the greatest possible number of native shipping and seamen. Our Coasting Trade has best answered this valuable purpose, by breeding the greatest number of excellent seamen, who by returning the most frequently into port, may be soonest had when their services are wanted.

Irish ships and seamen were declared by the act of Navigation itself to be English ships and seamen, which was in this respect expresly re-enacted in 1778; and they are consequently entitled to the same privileges, and subject to the same services.

But in truth it does not appear, how the Regulations now proposed will have the effect of increasing the ships and seamen of Ireland to the extent which has been imagined.—The surplus produce of Europe, which Ireland
may

may have to spare after satisfying her domestic demands, may, as the Law now stands, be sent to England under a liberal construction of the Act of Navigation and the established practice. This branch of Commerce will therefore undergo no alteration.—Ireland has not yet engaged in the African Trade.—She will not probably enter into a successful competition in it with Liverpool: From this source, therefore, Ireland is not likely to have soon any surplus to spare.

During the six years that she has enjoyed the West India Trade, she has not yet supplied her own consumption; for there were exported from England to Ireland

  In 1774, of Sugar, 172,406 Cwt.
  In 1784, of Ditto, 160,083 Cwt.

  In 1774, of Rum, 363,822 Gallons.
  In 1784, of Ditto, 944,479 Gallons.

And nearly in the same proportion of other West India Produce.

Ireland has therefore to smuggle for such a consumption as the foregoing, before she can send the articles into England to advantage;—the chances of the prices being accidentally lower here will never be an inducement, as the Markets fluctuate almost daily: Sugars therefore shipped at Cork or Waterford, with a view to a better price in London, Bristol or Liverpool, may come to a worse market than at home, with all the charges of freight, insurance, Custom-house fees, and waste, which last is considerable.

It may be worth enquiring how the Irish are to procure the Sugars, which some persons are so apprehensive will be sent through Ireland to Britain. They must get the West India produce, either by consignment or purchase.

If the Planter chooses to consign his Sugars to Ireland with a view to selling them, he may do it now; but he will never send them there in order to come afterwards to this Country. Will the Planter, who is now very frequently under covenant to consign his Sugars to his Merchant, from whom in such cases he expects advances, send his Sugars to Ireland, where he can expect little credit? Or, will any Planter consign his produce to Ireland, where it must be sold at six months credit, in preference to England, where it is fold at a lefs rifque, payable in two months? Glafgow has never had many confignments, becaufe, like Ireland, her Market is narrow. The Irifh then muft purchafe the Sugars which they want. It is calculated, that one Cargo of Irifh produce, will purchafe only half the lading of the fhip which carried it out; the other half muft be purchafed with bills, for which an Indorfer muft be found at the expence of two pounds and an half per cent. The Provifions always go to a precarious Market in the Weft Indies: The Sugars, which is liable to a great wafte and other damages, alfo comes to a precarious Market in Europe; and it is a fact, that owing to the beforementioned caufes, the Weft India Trade has already proved almoft as fatal to the Irifh Merchants, as the American Trade has done to the Traders of France.

The Irifh Merchant who had it in his power to bring the produce of the colonies directly to this Country, was enabled under Lord North's Law to invoice a Cargo to be delivered part at Cork or Waterford, and part at Briftol or London; is it then poffible to conceive, that under the propofed extenfion, he will import circuitoufly after a landing in Ireland, under all the difadvantages of double freight, infurances, Cuftom-houfe fees, &c. &c. &c. as before obferved, what fhe can now import directly?

Confidering then how much Ireland already enjoys under the conceffions of the laft feven years, the allowing her to re-fhip her furplus Sugars to Britain, is a boon fcarcely worth a conteft. Confidering too, that her Sugars muft thus come into competition with the Sugars directly imported, there is furely not much ground for apprehenfion.

The queftion as to the Act of Navigation may be thus briefly fummed up: From former conceffions, the Trade of Ireland is free to Foreign Nations; it is only limited as to her Sifter Kingdom. European produce fhe may now fend here; the produce of Africa and the Weft-Indies fhe cannot fend, if fhe had them. If Ireland gains no more by her American Trade than France, who is ftill obliged to buy Tobacco in London, fhe will not foon have much Colony produce to fpare: for although fhe has fome local advantages, fhe is infinitely behind France in Means of purchafing, and in Credit.

What

What valid reason can be given, then, for with-holding the little that on this head of the business is asked, making, as it does, a part of a whole System, which will secure to this Country a constant and increasing assistance towards defraying the general expences of the Empire. To judge of this prospect, it is worth while to state, that the hereditary Revenue, the surplus of which is to be appropriated to this purpose, produced, in the year ending at Lady-day last, 659,000l. which in 1684 amounted to no more than 234,076l. as appears by a Manuscript in the Harleian Collection. During the late Peace it continued increasing from 586,369l. in 1763, to 694,961l. in 1777.

If Ireland increased thus rapidly in her resources during the long period of her oppression, what may we not expect the produce to be when she is relieved therefrom.

It is impossible to review the general heads of this revenue without perceiving that the Trade, Manufactures, or Population of Ireland cannot increase, without the effect being felt in the proportionable augmentation of that Revenue: The only supposition, therefore, on which it can be imagined that nothing considerable will arise from it to the general support of the Empire, must be, that Ireland will derive no advantages from this Arrangement, or from the benefits of which she is now in possession.

Upon the whole of this interesting business, let it be considered, that it is now undertaken, for the first time, to obtain a final settlement of every great Commercial Point between the two countries; that this is brought forward upon the most mature deliberation, and on the fullest investigation; and let every impartial man decide, when he has seen all the Evidence which is to be offered in support of the Arrangement, whether it will be most for the advantage of this country to acquiesce with a settlement which must necessarily unite the two Countries for ever, and promote their mutal advantage, rendering Ireland a source of wealth and strength to this country; or to reject it, and abide by all the ill consequences which will follow to both the kingdoms, by a revival of jealousies, contentions, and jarring interests.

THE

APPENDIX.

THE ARRANGEMENTS WITH IRELAND CONSIDERED.

THE spirit of commerce, by making the many less dependent on the few, gradually overturned the massy fabric of the feudal constitutions. The progress of this spirit has, even in the short period of the present century, softened the temper of every European government. And it was the silent prevalence of this spirit, more perhaps than the avowed operations of design, which, during late times, prompted so many requests on the part of Ireland, and dictated so many grants by Great-Britain.

That much has been asked at different times and much has been given will not be regretted by those, who wish to see fellow-subjects enjoy privileges; or by those, who value above all things the blessings of domestic quiet within a convulsed Empire. It is only to be lamented, that what was at last done, was not decisively done, on the fair principles of mutual advantage and lasting contentment.

If we briefly review the restraints, which had been imposed formerly by our mercantile avarice more than by our jealousy; if we shortly consider the relief which has been given, during the last seven years, by our apprehensions, more than by our policy; if we compare the extent of what Ireland actually enjoys with the little that is now withheld; we shall see the truth of that regret in the best light, and probably determine, that there is now nothing in contest between the sister kingdoms, which can possibly counter-balance the disagreeableness of future altercation, the pleasures of promised concord, and the profit of equal industry, directed to one common end.

In 1778, which may be regarded as the period of rigour and the beginning of conceſſion, the produce of Ireland, except woollens, cottons, and hats, glaſs, hops, gunpowder and coals, were allowed to be exported* to the Britiſh Colonies in America, and to the Britiſh ſettlements in Africa: Iron too was permitted, on paying ſpecified duties. And foreign manufactures, which had been imported through England into Ireland for her own conſumption, were equally allowed to be tranſported to the ſame diſtant markets.

To enable us to judge of the value of what was then given, or withheld, we ought to recollect, that this act only reſtored ancient rights, without conferring new ones. All this and more might have been lawfully done from the commencement of colonization to the epoch of the Reſtoration: All this was permitted to be done, by the act of navigation itſelf †. Even the law, which in the firſt inſtance, excluded Ireland from the unreſtrained trade of our diſtant dominions, allowed ſervants, horſes and victuals to be ſent from Ireland to our colonies ‡; and to theſe articles linens were added by the 3 and 4 of An. ch. 8.—If we reflect, that the Iriſh exports of proviſions and linen alone amounted yearly to 3,250,000*l*. while the annual value of the whole exported products of Ireland was only 3,500,000*l*. ‖; we ſhall not probably think, that many of the reſtraints on that eſſential right of every community, to make the moſt of its own advantages, were even then withdrawn.

When the embargoes and embarraſſments of the war filled up at length the meaſure of Ireland's diſtreſſes; when the Iriſh aſked plainly for a free trade as an adequate relief from commercial burdens, we relinquiſhed much, but did not grant a free trade.

In 1779 indeed, we had allowed the importation of tobacco, being the growth of Ireland, under the like duties and regulations as American tobacco, when imported into Britain. A regard to our own manufactures more than to theirs, had induced us at the ſame time to grant a bounty on the import of Iriſh hemp into this kingdom§.

But

---

* By 18 Geo. III. ch. 55. But the articles, which were then excepted were allowed by the 20 Geo. III. chap. 10, for opening the Colony Trade.
† See 12 Ch. 2. ch. 18.
‡ By 15 Ch. 2. ch. 7.
‖ See Mr. Young's Tour in Ireland, Appen. p. 144.
§ By 19 Geo. III. Ch. 37.

APPENDIX. 23

But it was not till 1780, that after much delay, without much confideration, we reftored to Ireland an equal trade to the Britifh colonies in Africa and America*; including the export of her woollens, which it had been the object of fo many laws to prevent. We allowed too a direct commerce between Ireland and the Levant, by perfons free of the Levant Company. And the gold and filver coins, which the Irifh abfentees were fuppofed to have brought into England were now permitted to be fent back to Ireland †.

This then is the amount of what may be called Lord North's conceffions to Ireland. Whatever difadvantage may have refulted from them to Britain he merits the blame:—Whatever good flowed from them to Ireland he equally deferves her praife. Certain however it is, that after all, Ireland did not enjoy compleatly the plantation trade: For a people, who cannot difpofe of the commodities, which remain after domeftic confumption is fatisfied, cannot confume at the cheapeft rate; fince every ultimate difadvantage muft be confidered by the fupplier both in buying and felling: Now, Ireland was ftill reftrained, by an act ‡ paffed only eight years before, from fending out of her own ports the colony produce to Britain. The domeftic manufacturers of Ireland continued ftill to be loaded with many burdens, and her traffick with foreign countries to be prevented by a thoufand obftructions. To take away with one hand what is given by the other, can never merit the praife of liberality, however it may be contemned as equally inconfiftent with plain dealing as it is with found policy.

Amidft her fubfequent embarraffments Ireland thought, what no one who loves freedom will blame h for thinking, that fhe could manage beft her own affairs her own way. With this view, fhe afked for a free Legiflature; for a parliament over which no other parliament fhould be paramount. And Mr. Fox propofed in 1782, and caufed to be enacted a law ‖ for repealing the ftatute of the 6th of Geo. I. which fecured the dependency of Ireland. But, with all his renown for promptitude and decifivenefs he did not grant all that was afked, or at leaft what was regarded in Ireland as effectual to the end.

D 2 And

---

* By 20 Geo. III, ch. 10.
† For all which fee 20 Geo. III. ch. 18.
‡ 12 Geo. III. ch. 55.
‖ 22 Geo. III. ch. 53.

And he once more essayed his legislative talents, by carrying through in the subsequent year, an * act for declaring, *that the right claimed by the people of Ireland to be bound by laws made in their own Parliament, and to have all law-suits decided finally in their own courts, shall be established for ever.* The declaration made thus to Ireland, *that your legislature shall in future be free*, though a simple proposition, contained many consequences, that were by no means apparent to every one, and that were perhaps not all foreseen, by the author of the Irish revolution. For, the energy of the British legislature being thus withdrawn, all British acts of legislation ceased to operate in Ireland: Neither restrictions nor facilities, which had flowed from a fountain, that no longer flowed, could any more administer either good or evil to Ireland. If any mischief has resulted to Britain from these measures, Mr. Fox merits the blame; whatever benefits have resulted to Ireland he equally merits her commendations. We shall probably find by no long enquiry, that some advantages and many inconveniencies did result from the before-mentioned measures; owing to a real want of foresight in the authors of them, and to the consequent want of system, both in the object and the means.

The change itself may have indeed produced some inconvenience to Ireland first, and to Britain afterwards. But, it was the inadequateness of the inconsiderate modes to the before-mentioned ends, which gave rise to the recent disputes and dangers, both commercial and political. Lord North (as we have seen) avowedly opened to Ireland the trade to our Colonies: Mr. Fox virtually extended the Irish commerce with foreign nations: yet, both these ministers left the trade and navigation between the Sister Kingdoms, which, considering their relationship and proximity, ought to be the most free, obnoxious to many disputes, and liable to some obstructions. The Irish naturally inferred, that when a thing is given, all must necessarily be given, without which the same thing cannot be enjoyed. When they found moreover their Portugal trade embarrassed, their jealousy traced up the cause to the same temper, which, after pretending to give the whole had only given a part. They feared, that the admitting freely into Britain without a duty the provisions of Ireland would operate as a tax upon their own consumption. They complained, that
the

the prohibiting by high duties the importation of their woollens and other stuffs into Britain, while they excluded from their markets foreign goods of the same kind, shewed a disposition to oppress, without benefitting the oppressors themselves: and that the allowing of drawbacks on the export of British refined sugars, sailcloth and cottons, amounted to a tax on their inconsiderable manufactures of the same kind. To quiet these complaints, by removing or obviating the chief cause of them, no provision seems to have been made either by Lord North, or Mr. Fox; since no inquiries were certainly made by either of them into the real state of the manufactures of both countries, in order to remove the jealousies of tradesmen, by putting the manufactures and business of all upon an equitable footing; and by getting in return some security for future satisfaction.

To the before-mentioned causes may be truly referred the desire of protecting duties and equalizing drawbacks, which have been insisted on, together with associations of non-importation of British manufactures, which were actually executed with no small effect, when legal modes of redress had been denied. And while Britain began to enjoy all the blessings of returning peace, Ireland fell back into an abyss of deeper distractions, and seemed ready to seek relief even from the miseries of civil war.

The disturbances of Ireland, which thus plainly arose from large concessions without previous concert, and from a positive admission of independence without any agreement of future aid, were bequeathed with other similar legacies by the late ministers to the present. Of this state the whole nation felt the unhappiness, and every one wished for an investigation of the true causes of those disorders, that effectual remedies might be sought. The wishes of the public were doubtless complied with, by much inquiry first, and by much consideration afterwards. Were we to judge from actual effects more than from public report, we may infer, that those persons who knew best the affairs of Ireland and were intrusted with her interests, have been consulted with regard to the origin of the disease as well as to the efficacy of the cure.

Of the Irish Parliament it cannot be asserted, as of the American Congress, that when oppressed by their grievances they declined to trace up their sufferings to the true source, to avow their real object, and to point out plainly such means as would be fully adequate to the end

of

of removing real distress and preventing after jealousies. To justify this remark it is unnecessary to recapitulate the addresses of the Irish Parliament, during the last seven years. It is sufficient to mention the Resolves, which were entered into, on the 7th of February, 1785, by the Irish Commons, with such apparent sincerity and zeal, *for encouraging and extending the trade between Great Britain and Ireland, and for settling the intercourse and commerce between them on permanent and equitable principles, in order to promote the mutual benefit of both countries.*

Whether these are objects of the highest importance to the general interest of the British Empire, what unprejudiced person can doubt? As the Parliamentary Resolutions of a sister kingdom, they merit the highest attention; as proposals directed to the most useful end, they deserve the most candid discussion; and as measures which lead directly to the peaceful settlement of a distracted Empire upon a digested plan of systematic government, these proposals ought to be supported by every wise and good man, were they less just in their principle and less salutary in their means.

Though the specifick proposals of the Irish Parliament have been detailed, for the sake of perspicuity, into ten resolutions, they may be considered under three distinct heads: 1st, As they tend to affect our domestic manufactures; 2dly, As they will probably enlarge or diminish the foreign trade of both; and 3dly, as the public burthen may be lightened at present, or lessened in future, were these resolves substantially adopted. It is proposed to speak briefly of each of these points, according to the foregoing arrangement.

1. Whether admitting the products and manufactures of the sister kingdom mutually into each other, without paying any other duty than the lowest duty, which may be payable on importation in either country, except where an internal duty may have already been imposed on the same article of the importing country, is doubtless a question of great importance, which merits serious discussion. The general proposal plainly is, that the products and manufactures of both kingdoms shall be mutually imported and consumed, with as little burthen, and as equally as possible. And to this it is objected: *That the advantage of cheap provisions, low wages, and no taxes, must enable*

the

the Irish manufacturer to underfell the English at every market, not excepting our own, particularly in woollens. The objector evidently borrowed his documents from Lord Sheffield's *Observations on the Irish Trade*, without adverting, how clearly the noble author hath proved, that at the time Ireland, on the opening of her ports for exportation of woollens, made an effort to fend the greateſt quantity to foreign markets, ſhe increaſed her imports of woollens from England: That Ireland is hardly in a ſituation to agree to that propoſal; as Great Britain could underſell her in moſt manufactures; ſuch is the predominancy of ſuperior ſkill, induſtry and capitals, over low priced labour, and comparatively very few taxes*. The queſtion then is anſwered, as far as Lord Sheffield may be allowed to anſwer it.

But let us attend to the reaſon of the thing. It is unneceſſary on this occaſion, to revive the famous controverſy; *Whether a poor country, where raw materials and proviſions are cheap, and wages low, can ſupplant the trade of a rich manufacturing country, where raw materials and proviſions are dear, and the price of labour high:* This point has been ſo decidedly ſettled in favour of the rich manufacturing country by Dean Tucker, that it can be now only brought forward by ignorance, or intereſt, or faction. Let us only conſider the caſe of two individual manufacturers ſettled in the ſame neighbourhood, a rich one and a poor one: The rich one, being already poſſeſſed of capital, credit, and cuſtomers, can plainly buy his materials at the cheapeſt rate, work them up in the beſt manner, becauſe he can give the beſt wages to the beſt workmen, and diſpoſe of his finiſhed goods more readily and lower than the poor one: If the rich manufacturer employs a capital of £.2000, and the poor one only £.200, the rich manufacturer, by gaining ten per cent. or £.200 a year, can live comfortably; but the poor tradeſman muſt gain 20 per cent. or £.40 a year, before he can live at all: Conſequently the rich manufacturer muſt be always able to underſell the poor one 10 per cent. on every article. Every manufacturer, however opulent and eſtabliſhed he may now be, muſt remember the many difficulties he had to encounter in his youth, when he met his richer neighbour in every market, whether in buying

* See *Obſervations on the Iriſh Trade*, p. 13, 19.

buying his materials, in employing the moſt expert workmen, or in ſelling his goods: And he may recollect perhaps with pleaſure, that it required a life of patience, attention, and induſtry, to ſurmount every difficulty, attending a too powerful competition, and to become himſelf rich.

A manufacturing town is compoſed of ſuch individuals, whoſe active competitions promote the proſperity and riches of their neighbourhood. A ſimilar competition may prevail between a rich manufacturing town and a poor one: But, has Bolton yet overcome Mancheſter? Has Roachdale overpowered Leeds? or has Walſal eclipſed the ſkill, and induſtry, and opulence of Birmingham? It is on the other hand known and underſtood, that all the little towns, which ſtand within ten miles circle of Mancheſter, Leeds, and Birmingham, are the mere inſtruments belonging to theſe capitals of their reſpective manufactures.

Of ſuch towns and villages is a manufacturing province or kingdom compoſed; who may in the ſame manner, as a province or kingdom, enter into competition with each other. But, has Wales or Scotland, notwithſtanding their ſuppoſed advantages of cheap materials and low-priced labour, yet carried away the Woollen Manufacture from England? The truth is, England was and is in poſſeſſion (a point of great conſequence in every thing) of ſuperior wealth, which ſhe had gained, not by war, or by mines of gold and ſilver, but by ages of attention and induſtry; of eſtabliſhed credit and extenſive correſpondences; of the ſkill and experience, that reſulted from all theſe; and of the diviſion of labour, which naturally takes place in the progreſs of manufacture, and which enables the workmen not only to labour ſkilfully but to ſell cheaply.

Of all theſe advantages Ireland is doubtleſs in ſome degree poſſeſt. But, the nature of the queſtion ſuppoſes a great inferiority, otherwiſe there would be no reaſon for apprehenſion. Of the ſtate of Ireland, in reſpect of lowneſs of labour, habits of induſtry, cheapneſs of living, and extent of capital, it may be proper however to inquire a little more minutely.

If it is allowed, that there are two million and a half of people in Ireland; it will be equally admitted that the two millions are Roman Catholics, and that the half million

tion are Proteſtants. The Proteſtants reſide chiefly in the North, and are principally employed in carrying on the Linen Manufactures. It is a remarkable fact in the œconomy of theſe tradeſmen, that each occupies a little farm, which he cultivates in due ſeaſon, though he may be obliged to ſtop the loom, in order to follow the plough. And his capital and his time are conſequently directed to a different employment from his real buſineſs. He is therefore neither ſo good a farmer, nor manufacturer, as if he employed his undivided attention and money to one object. This fact alone evinces, that induſtry has not ariſen to that ſtate of improvement, even among the moſt induſtrious of the Iriſh manufacturers, which reſults from the diviſion of labour; conſiſting as this happy circumſtance does, in the workmen applying attentively to one buſineſs only and even ſolely to one branch of this buſineſs. But, no cheapneſs of labour can compenſate for the beforementioned diſtraction of employment: And no attention and ſkill can enter into conteſt for cheapneſs with the machines which have been introduced into England; as we may learn from the deciſive ſucceſs of the great works for the ſpinning of cotton. The price of wages have riſen about one fourth *, during the laſt twenty years, in both kingdoms; which remarkable fact ſufficiently evinces, that both hold an equal pace in improvements and in wealth. Common labour is little more than one third of what it is in England; yet it is very extraordinary, that maſons, carpenters, thatchers, and ſuch artizans ſhould be paid nearly as much in Ireland as in England; though it muſt be acknowledged, that the wages of manufacture is a good deal lower in Ireland than in England; while the rates of living are in the firſt country to the laſt as eleven to fourteen. But, in forming ſuch eſtimates we ought always to conſider whether ſuperior ſkill and induſtry are not an ample compenſation for higher wages. The common ditcher of Norfolk would be a cheaper labourer at eighteen pence a day, than the ſtouteſt Patagonian at twopence. If Ireland, from whatever cauſe, ſhould in future advance in her trade and manufactures with quicker ſteps than Britain, the price of wages will riſe in the ſame proportion; becauſe it is not the actual wealth in any country which raiſes the value of labour; but the greater demand for labour from frequent employment. The competition, which will ſoon ariſe between the linen and woollen manufacturers,

* Mr. Young's Tour, Appen.

turers, between the workers in silk and workers in cotton, must necessarily raise the price of every kind of labour: For, workmen never fail to pursue that business, which brings them the greatest wages. Two very important truths ought however never to be forgotten, in forming such comparisons: the general industry of no people can ever exceed what their capital can employ; no regulation of commerce can any where increase the quantity of industry, beyond what the capital of the country can maintain; though such a regulation may divert the employment of it to a business less advantageous than that to which it would have naturally gone; several examples of which may be found in Ireland.

The foregoing reasonings and facts apply chiefly to the manufacturing Protestants of Ireland. With regard to the great body of Irish people, the Roman Catholicks, it has been justly remarked, that the whole tenor of the Irish law necessarily tended not so much to convert them from their errors, as to beggar their fortunes; to depress them by a sense of hopeless penury; and to render them indolent and inattentive by putting them in constant remembrance, that they could not better their condition by any efforts. But, the prevalence of liberality had induced the legislatures of both kingdoms to relax a little in their favour. And the Roman Catholicks of Ireland may now take leases, or buy lands, though not even now with the freedom of Protestants. The desire of every man to become an owner of a portion of his country is the great realizer of mercantile capital. Whether the late freedom, which has been justly given to the Roman Catholicks, will therefore promote the advantage of agriculture, or the interests of manufacture, in Ireland, may admit of some doubt. A very competent judge has certainly determined * after great enquiry, that money laid out upon the improvement of the unimproved lands of Ireland would yield from fifteen to twenty per cent. profit, besides other advantages. But, amidst the present competitions of the mercantile world, what merchant or manufacturer, can expect to make more than ten per cent. by his business? It would however require (according to the same judge) five pounds sterling to be expended upon every acre English, amounting to 88,341,136*l.*

to

Mr. A. Young's Tour in Ireland, Append. p. 20.

to build, fence, drain, plant and improve Ireland, in the same manner as the face of England is improved. It would require twenty shillings an acre more, amounting to above twenty millions, to stock the farms of Ireland, like those of England. Here then is a permanent drain, which may carry off the whole accumulations of the mercantile capital of Ireland and probably will draw off many of them. Happy for Ireland will it be, if she shall thus lay out the surplusses of her stock, in improving her own fields, in preference to the more splendid and precarious expenditure on West-India estates. Nor is this evil much to be dreaded by the Irish patriot, or feared by the English partyman. The Irish Parliament, by giving bounties on the land-carriage of corn to Dublin, have incited a vigorous spirit of tillage, though to the diminution indeed of pasturage and the loss of manufacture. It is not likely then that the mercantile surplusses of Irish stock will soon accumulate faster than those of British stock. Were we to suppose, what might easily be proved, that the mercantile capital of Britain is to the mercantile capital of Ireland as an hundred is to one: Were we to suppose, that the mercantile capitals of both increase with the vigour of compound interest: It would surely require no deep calculation to prove, how much faster the capital of Britain must necessarily augment than the capital of Ireland.

It is nevertheless said by some, and feared by others, that were we to ratify the mutual freedom of manufacture, which the Irish have proposed, the labour, the skill, and capital of Britain would emigrate to Ireland. If it be thereby meant, that the mere artificers would retire to Ireland to get less wages than they now receive at home, this is surely no probable supposition. If it be imagined, that the most skilful artisans would be tempted by high rewards to manage the manufactures of Ireland and instruct the ignorant, this is only saying, that the Irish will do that hereafter, which they have always done, without perceiveably injuring British fabricks; because in proportion to the charges of the master, must the goods be enhanced to the consumer; and it has been seldom found from experience, that the tradesman, who has been tempted from his native country by high wages, has long preserved his morals. He who asserts, that mercantile capital may easily be transferred from one country to another, has perhaps no clear conception what mercantile capital is. Credit, and correspondences, are as much capital as cash. Every manufacture may certainly carry off his cash: But, he cannot transport with him to a strange land the good opinion of his neighbours, from which he derived so many benefits in the purchase of his raw materials; or the favours of his customers, which formed the chief vent for his finished goods. The Protestant weavers of Ireland, who used to emigrate to America (the Roman Catholicks never emigrated) are said to have carried away large sums of money; but, they transported nothing else: They found themselves among strangers, without credit or friends. And they retired into the wilderness, where they followed the plough, but forgot the loom. He who has made a capital, by pursuing a particular object will not quit that object to look for another: He who has inherited a capital from the industry of his father, will not send his property to a place where he does not chuse to reside. And were we to appeal to experience we should probably be convinced, that no capital having been sent to cut the canals or work the collieries of Ireland, which have so long languished, notwithstanding public support, none will be transmitted in future for similar purposes.

But with regard to the general subject, a few authentic facts will be more satisfactory than a thousand speculations. The linen trade between the sister kingdoms, has, for almost a century, existed in that free and equal state, which is now proposed for every other product, and manufacture of both. Yet, British linens have flourished notwithstanding the unlimitted competition of the Irish; as we may infer from the subjoined details * :

	Imported	Re-exported
According to a 5 years average ending with 1756, there were	31,561,536 yds.	7,524,346 yds.
Ditto ending with 1771, only	24,988,477	8,245,793

And thus it appears, that the domestic manufacture encreased, by the diminution of the quantity of linen, which was imported, and by the augmentation of the quantity, which

* Reports of the Linen Committee, quoted by Mr. A. Young, in Pol. Arithmetic, p. 315-16.

which was afterwards sent out. A good deal of British linen was sent to Ireland. But, the encreafe of the British linens, notwithſtanding the Iriſh competition, will appear ſtill plainer, from a fair compariſon of the quantities of Britiſh and Iriſh linens, which have been exported from England.

	Britiſh Linens.	Iriſh Linens.
According to a ſeven years average, ending with 1755	576,373,yds.	772,245
Ditto ending with 1762	1,355,266	1,985,825
Ditto ending with 1769	2,423,664	2,033,444
in 1770	3,210,506	2,707,482
in 1771	4,411,040	3,450,224

The foregoing detail ſhews clearly enough that the Britiſh linens have greatly proſpered, though they had the Iriſh for unreſtrained competitors, and even entered into competition with the Iriſh in the Iriſh markets. And this deciſive truth will ſtill more plainly appear, from a more minute ſtatement of the Scots linen, becauſe Scotland is much more analogous to Ireland, in her ſkill, induſtry, and capital, than England. An Act of Parliament was paſſed in 1727, for encouraging the linen manufacture in Scotland. From that epoch the progreſs of this valuable manufacture has been prodigious, as appears from the ſubjoined detail *.

		Yards.
Linen ſtamped for ſale in Scotland according to a 5 years average, ending with	1733	3,488,232
Ditto	1742	4,673,373
Four years ending	1751	7,543,075
in	1754	8,914,369
in	1774	11,422,115

Yet the Iriſh linens, amounting to fifteen million of yards, entered freely into competition with the Scots, in the domeſtic market, and were entitled to the ſame bounties on the exportation. And this ſeems to be a fair anſwer of the queſtion, by actual experiment, the beſt of all trials.

It having in this ſatisfactory manner appeared, that the Britiſh manufacturers have nothing to fear from the competition of the Iriſh fabricks, it is proper to enquire, what are the proper manufactures of Ireland, which may be imported

* And. Chron. Com. 2 vol. p. 400-9.

ported into Britain, even as the law now stands: We shall immediately find, that linen, and linen yarn, bay yarn, cotton yarn, beef, pork, bacon, butter, hydes, calf-skins, and live cattle, may be imported from Ireland duty free: That woollen cloths, stuffs of silks and cotton rugs, and fringe may be brought in, on paying a duty: And that cheese, and salt, unless for ships use, are alone prohibited.

Of the first class, namely, such articles as may even now be legally imported, whatever may be their value (and their value amounts to nineteen twentieths of the whole imported) there is at present no dispute, since experience hath decided in their favour.

As to the second class, consisting of woollen cloths; of stuffs of silk and cotton; and of rugs and frizes; all these may be now imported into Britain, on paying a duty which amounts to a prohibition; the same articles are admitted into Ireland from Britain on paying a duty of 5 per cent. of the value; and foreign goods of the same kind are excluded from Ireland by prohibitory duties. It is apparent, that Ireland now may equally prohibit British woollens and admit the foreign, when she may get them cheaper; which answers the objection, *that we give every thing, and receive nothing in return.* True indeed, Britain may equally give a preference to foreign linens over the Irish. But, would such a contest be for the interest or happiness of Britain, or of Ireland? The true question then is, whether the woollens, cottons, or silks of Ireland, could rival the British in the markets of Britain, were they freely admitted, burdened only with freight and insurance, Custom-house fees and factorage, to the amount of 8 or 10 per cent. The general argument, whether the poor country can enter into successful rivalry with an opulent one, has been already discussed and plainly decided in favour of the rich Manufacturing Country. But, to leave no doubt on any one's mind, it is now necessary to examine the point more minutely as to the woollens, silks, and cottons of England and Ireland.

The general aspect of the manufactures of both countries appears to be this—The woollens predominate in Britain—The linens predominate in Ireland. From the plenty of the raw material and the encouragement of the legislature, the woollens of England, at an early epoch, took possession of the country and so fully occupied the industrious

dustrious classes that it always proved a too powerful competitor to the feebler fabrick of linen, of cotton, and of silk. On the other hand, the linen manufacture of Ireland, from the convenience of the country and the encouragement of the legislature has grown up to great magnitude, has fully employed the industrious classes there, however few they may be when compared with the whole people, and continues from its particular advantages to oppress the silk, the cotton, and woollen. The Irish woollens moreover labour under a considerable disadvantage peculiar to themselves. The whole island does not produce a sufficient quantity of wool to supply the home market. Owing to the public encouragements to agriculture the great sheep walks of Carlow, Tiperary, and Roscommon have been converted into tillage. And thus the quantity of wool, which was originally too little has by this means become less. Of consequence the price of wool in Ireland is from 45 to 50 per cent. higher than it is in England, the price being as about ten to six. In this country the value of the raw material is supposed to be about one third of the whole cost of the cloth: In that country the amount of the raw material is two thirds * of the whole charges of the manufacture. Here then is a natural and permanent disadvantage attending the woollen manufacture of Ireland, which can never be counter-balanced by the low price of labour, affected as it more and more must be by the competitions of linen, silk, and cotton fabrics, that are pressed forward in the same country. Under such disadvantages is it likely that the woollens of Ireland, can enter into successful competition with the woollens of England? If the linens of Ireland did not (as we have seen) depress the linens of Scotland, is it reasonable to conclude, that the woollens of Ireland can rival the woollens of England, which, notwithstanding the competition

of

---

* Mr. A. Young states the price of an Irish ball of Wool, during 1778, in this manner:

Combing and spinning	—	0 1 0¼
The wool	—	0 2 5¼
Whole cost		0 3 6

See much good information on this subject in his Irish Tour, the Appendix throughout.

of Europe, have arifen up to a vaft magnitude, fince the commencement of the prefent century; as we may learn more minutely from the fubjoined detail: The whole value of exported woollens, according to a five years

   Average, ending with 1705 £2,579,478
   Ditto   with 1775   4,344,942

It is however faid—*to be aftonifhing how Ireland has increafed her woollen trade within thefe few years.* It is doubtlefs true, that fince Lord North allowed the export of Irifh woollens to our Colonies, and Mr. Fox laid open the foreign trade of Ireland, fhe has exported thofe woollens openly, which fhe formerly did fecretly: And fhe manufactures now what fhe always manufactured, poplins and tabinets, which cannot rival England, while England fhall continue not to make them. But, it is an acknowledged fact, that while Ireland has been thus fending her peculiar woollens to foreigners, fhe has imported a greater quantity of Englifh woollens for her own wear. This decifive fact might be fufficiently proved (were any proof wanting) by the fubjoined detail:

	New Drapery. yds.	Old Drapery. yds.
Of Britifh woollens there were imported into Ireland, according to a feven years average, ending with 1770	331,548	205,662
Ditto according to a five years average ending the 25 March, 1784	376,719	316,625

This authentick account ought to outweigh a thoufand arguments and ought therefore to calm every apprehenfion on the fubject of woollens.

But, of Irifh filks and cottons little has yet been faid, far lefs proved. The Irifh have certainly tried to introduce and fupport thefe manufactures, during the two laft twenty years; though without much fuccefs. Had public boards in Ireland done lefs and private men been able to do more, the national efforts had been more fuccefsful. It is unneceffary to repeat arguments, which are equally applicable to cotton and filk, as they were before to woollen and linen. And every reafonable perfon will be fooner fatisfied

               by

by a fair appeal to facts. With this purpose the following details are submitted to every ones judgements:—

There were imported from England into Ireland, according to a thirteen years average ending with — 1764—15,760—48,132— 275
Ditto with — 1777—18,200—45,990—1,068
Five years aver. with Mar. 1784—19,164—41,606—1,588

(Manufac. lb. Raw silk. lb. Ribband turned silk. lb.)

There were imported into Ireland of British manufactured linen, cotton, and silk, according to a seven years average, ending with — 1770—£16,784
Ditto ending with ———— 1777— 25,208
Ditto 5 years ending with March — 1784— 88,948

The foregoing details by no means exhibit the Irish manufactures of cotton and silk in an increasing state; though some, if not all of the five last years were a good deal lessened by the non-importation agreements of the Irish populace. It is the laudable object of the late proposals to prevent in future all such irregular modes of redress or fluctuation of Trade, by removing present grievances and preventing future ones. We may judge what expectations are formed from the adoption of these proposals, by a fact, which is very well understood on Change, that there are considerable orders for British goods now in the city from Ireland to be executed on the supposition, that the equity of these proposals will ensure their acceptance.

Having thus minutely examined the great branches of the trade with Ireland, without touching the smaller ones, it may be now proper to take a flight but satisfactory view of our general commerce, with Ireland, both before the Irish were allowed to traffick with all the world, and since.

	Value of Exports.	Value of Imports.
There were exported and imported to and from England and Ireland, goods valued, according to a ten year average, ending with 1770	£.1,818,595	£.1,032,436
Ditto with 1780	1,897,001	1,412,130
Ditto in 1781	1,782,364	1,433,788
in 1782	1,665,531	1,348,559
in 1783	2,161,815	1,499,229

Now, what is there in this view of a great subject, from the Custom-house books, that can discourage any one? And the foregoing reasonings and authentic facts, have been thus submitted to the reader's judgement, to enable him to determine how far the manufactures of Ireland can enter into effectual competition with the similar manufactures of Britain, loaded as the Irish must come to market, with additional charges, to no small amount.

2. It is proposed in the next place to consider, how far the foreign trade of both kingdoms is likely to be affected by the late proposals, were they adopted, as the means of promoting the permanent interest of both countries.

We shall both shorten the enquiry, and more easily comprehend the reasoning, if we throw out of the question every thing which does not belong to it.

The Irish may now trade with the British Plantations in Africa and America, from Lord North's commercial concessions. This point is not disputed. From Mr. Fox's political concessions, the Irish may regulate and pursue their commerce with foreign powers, as they may think it convenient to themselves. Of this there can be no doubt. Having in pursuance of this right imported any of the products of Europe, the Irish may afterwards export such products to Britain; under a decided construction of the act of navigation, and the established practice, subsequent to such decision. Of this then there can be no dispute. Under Lord North's concessions too, the Irish may import part of a cargo from the British West Indies, and sent forward the other part of it in the same ship to Britain. Neither is there any hesitation about this practice. What is it then that the Irish cannot do under the present laws? They cannot it seems import directly the produce of Africa and America into Ireland, and send it, after being there put on shore, to any British port: This therefore is all that they cannot at present lawfully do: And from this restriction they would doubtless be freed, were the proposed regulations adopted.

Among the thousand evils, wherewith the removing of this vexatious restraint from a free trade, is said to be pregnant, the principal one is, *That it would overthrow the act of navigation.* Were the Irish proposals to be attended with any such consequence, it would indeed be a serious objection to them. But, in order to determine properly, whether this is a valid objection, or a mere pretence,

tence, let us take two diſtinct views of the navigation act; 1ſt, As its principle and proviſions have a tendency to promote the foreign trade and domeſtic opulence of the people ; and 2dly, As its principle and proviſions tend to create many ſhips and ſailors, as a nurſery, from which future navies may be manned.

As to the firſt view of this important ſubject; it need ſcarcely be remarked, that Sir Mathew Decker conſidered the act of navigation as a mere monopoly, which ought to be removed, to make way for a freer trade. For, he inſiſted, that by confining the freights to one ſet of men; namely, Britiſh ſhipping and ſailors, imported goods were neceſſarily ſold dearer, and the products of the country, which were to be ſent out, were in the ſame manner likely to be purchaſed, by the exporter, ſo much cheaper. Doctor Adam Smith, has argued the point nearly in the ſame manner, without ſpeaking ſo bluntly. If foreigners are hindered from coming to ſell, they cannot always, ſays he, afford to come to buy ; becauſe if they come without a cargo, they muſt loſe the freight from their own country. By thus diminiſhing the number of ſellers, we thereby leſſen the number of buyers, and may in this manner be obliged not only to buy foreign goods dearer, but to ſell our own cheaper, than if there was a perfect freedom of trade. Yet, as defence, continues this judicious writer, is of more importance than riches, the act of navigation is perhaps the wiſeſt of all the commercial regulations of England ; though *it is not favourable to foreign commerce, or to the growth of that opulence which may ariſe from it.*

The reaſonings and authority of theſe able writers were placed in this broad light, in order to abate if poſſible, the confidence of thoſe, who expect that the monopoly of the freight and factorage created by the act of navigation, is to make Britain ſuperlatively rich ; and to expoſe the raſhneſs of any man, who can be ſo ill adviſed as vehemently to maintain* : That *The depreciation of landed eſtates, and the ruin of ſtock-holders, and of public credit, would be among the certain conſequences of what ?* — of allowing ſubjects to ſend in Britiſh ſhips, any little ſurplus of American products, that may remain after the domeſtic conſumption of Ireland may be ſatisfied. For this can be the ſole effect of the propoſed regulations. The truth then is,

* See Lord Sheffield on the Iriſh Trade.

is, that the vast augmentation of the riches of Britain, during the effluxion of the last hundred years, did not arise from the act of navigation, but, in spite of this law; which was enacted for a quite different and more valuable purpose, namely, the naval defence of the country.

But, let us inquire a little more minutely how the proposed regulation would probably affect the planters, or, producers of West India goods, in the first place, and the people at large, or the consumers, in the second place.

The monopoly, by which all the products of the Colonies were restrained for sale by the British markets, has been always complained of by the planters, because it plainly lessened the price of their sugars, and other products, by narrowing their market; and by excluding consequently a number of buyers. And the planters, as it was natural, constantly endeavoured to procure a relaxation of the monopoly, and thereby to augment the number of their customers. The consumers were equally injured by the monopoly, whereby they were confined to one set of suppliers, by the exclusion of foreign sugars, which necessarily raised the price. The West India planters had the address to procure, in 1738, a law * for allowing them to send their sugars to every market in Europe, first in British *built* ships, and afterwards in British *owned* ships, for a limited time, which will expire in September, 1785. Out of this law Ireland was still excepted. By thus enlarging the markets, and gaining a new set of customers, it was expected, that the value of the commodity would be raised. Under this law, the sugars, which had been sent to Hamburgh (for example) might be afterwards sent to Petersburgh. This too was beneficial for the planter, because he was thereby enabled to try another market.

Now, it would have still been more beneficial to have sent also the sugars to London, when this great market happened to be the highest of all, had the law allowed him to do so.

It is worth while to consider, what would be the effect were we to enlarge the beforementioned law, so as to enable the British planter to bring his sugars, which he may have sent to foreign ports, from thence to London in British ships. If we could provide, by whatever means, that foreign sugars should not mingle with our own, the interest

of

---

* 12 Geo. 2. ch. 30 15 G. 2. ch. 33. 18 G. 3. ch. 45.

of the planter would by such a measure be promoted by having another chance of sale. The interest of British consumers would be something promoted, by having a greater quantity of goods brought to the domestic market. And the interest of the public would be also promoted by the employment of a greater number of British shipping and sailors. Add to which, that if even *foreign* sugars were by this means mingled with British sugars, the interest of the consumers would be still more promoted, by lowering a little the price of the commodity; and the public by the still greater number of British ships, which would probably in this case be employed.

If it was advantageous to the planter to be permitted to send his sugar to every port in Europe, except to those of Ireland; he was surely allowed an additional advantage, when the ports of Ireland were also opened. If it would be advantageous to the planter, the consumer and the public, to admit British sugars, which had been sent in British ships to Hamburgh or Petersburgh to be re-shipped in British ships to Britain; it would be equally advantageous to the planter, to consumers, and the public, to allow British sugars to be sent in British ships from Ireland to Britain; which is the point that was to be proved.

Yet, some of the West India planters, though not all of them, have resolved, that allowing their own sugars to be re-shipped in British vessels to Britain, after being first landed in Ireland, would enable the Irish to smuggle French sugars into Ireland first and into Britain afterwards. Were this objection founded in probability it would doubtless justify the resolve as to the planters, though the consumers may still wish to get any sugars at the cheapest rate. It ought however to be remembered, that the French government does not wink at the sending clandestinely of sugars from the West Indies as they allow brandies to be sent from Dunkirk. We know, that in order to enforce rigorously the monopoly of their own sugars the French have lately seized some of the vessels of the American states, which they equally exclude, for attempting a practice that cannot easily be concealed. Let us however suppose, that the French governors were to shut their eyes and the French guard-ships to retire from their charge, it may be asked, what the Irish smuggler can carry to tempt the French planters to sell their

sugars

sugars clandestinely? Irish linens cannot be sold so cheap in the French islands as the French linens can, because they are not so good. Salted provisions may be always bought in open market. And consequently the Irish smuggler can carry nothing to the French West Indies that would purchase half a lading of sugars, considering how much they have lately risen in their price, and how much delay, risque, and expence there must be in putting them on board. Let us suppose the smuggled cargo safely arrived on the Irish coast, would the smuggler meet with no Custom-house cutters at sea and no Custom-house officers on shore. Here they would meet with Custom-house officers as vigilant and faithful, as they are any where to be found, as we might suppose from the late seizure of an East India ship, if the fact were not acknowledged by the whole mercantile world. Whether after all this risque and trouble the smuggler could undersell the fair trader in England, or in Ireland, is a point that ought to be considered by both parties.

It ought to be moreover remembered, that all this scene of smuggling may be acted as the law now stands, perhaps more easily than if all doubts and obstructions were removed from legal intercourse. The act of 12 George III, which is supposed to prohibit the sending of sugars from Ireland, was virtually repealed by Mr. Fox's law of 1782, as far as it was to operate in Ireland, though it continued in force as far as it was to operate in Britain. For any thing therefore, there is in that act (12 George III.) sugars may be cleared from the Custom-house in Ireland; though they cannot be entered in the Custom-house in Britain: The ship may sail for Britain; but she cannot come into port: She may hover in the channel, having a legal clearance on board; and she cannot consequently be seized by the cutters. If a law were to be made on purpose to furnish occasions to the smugglers, could any more favourable be given than those already given, by the present state of doubt and distraction. To remove these doubts and distractions is one of the proposed regulations. If sugars are sometimes smuggled from the French West Indies to the British by the planters, and afterwards shipped as their own; the planters themselves ought to look to such avaricious practices.

Let us assume then, since it has been well nigh proved, that to smuggle so unwieldy and wasteful an article as sugar, would

would be impossible, we may inquire, if in this case, it would be contrary to the interest of the grower to allow such sugar to be imported in British ships from Ireland to Britain, after it had been landed in Ireland: If he is a resident planter he can only dispose of his crop by sale or consignment, since barter is not practised. The Irish trader, who knows, that he cannot, after the home market is supplied, send the surplus to the best market, cannot afford so much for the goods, as if he knew that the vent was altogether free. Every detriment consequently, which is thrown in the way of him who buys to sell to the consumer, is a disadvantage to the producer. And it must ever be for the benefit of the grower to have many markets and various buyers, in order to have the convenience of competition. The planter who does not feel this to be his true interest does not know his interest.

On the other hand, if the grower inclines to consign his sugars, what ought to be his wish? to have his inclinations checked by a monopoly, or left free to range in quest of buyers; to have all the world before him, or to be confined to a single port. The West Indians were once confined to this island alone for the sale of their sugars. We have read of *the means of the plantations*, on this account. The West Indians *moaned* till they were allowed to send their sugars almost to every market in Europe. They *moan* now, because they are offered another chance for another market. We have read too of a people, who were offered freedom, yet refused it.

Leaving the planters to find out their true interest in this business we may be allowed to attend a little to the interests of that respectable body of men, the West India merchants. Their interest in these proposals is surely very plain: If the sugars are sent (as by law they now may be) to Ireland, and are there sold to the consumer, the commission must be lost to the British merchants: If such sugars should be thence sent to the better markets of Britain, the British merchants must necessarily get the commissions with the other advantages of the consignment. But it is insisted on behalf of these very merchants by Lord Sheffield, that this method of getting the consignment, (for the noble author is not arguing against sending the sugars directly from the place of their growth to Ireland) would *greatly weaken the security*, which they have on West India estates from money advanced: That is, in
other

other words, the giving of the traders another chance to get the produce of the estates into their own possession is to weaken their security. But, pray what is this same security? The paper and wax; or the judgment of law upon breach of contract; or last, though not least, the *interest* of the planter himself to continue his correspondence, in order by his punctuality to engage the merchant to accept his future bills, and to send him supplies, during every season; the *interest*, which the planter has to transmit his produce to the greatest market, rather than the smallest one.

On behalf of the whole nation the noble author objects, that admitting the before-mentioned surplusses of sugar from Ireland would deliver up the West India trade to the Irish. If we sift this objection, we shall find, that though it means well it means little. The interest of the British people, or consumers of sugars, consists in getting them at the cheapest rate from any place. The advantage of the planters, or producers, consists, in having the world for their market. And the benefit of the merchant, or middleman between the producers and consumers, arises out of his commission from both parties. The argument, as far as it goes to shew, that the British merchant would probably lose his commission, had been a good argument against Lord North's measure, whereby he delivered the sugars to the Irish: But, the Irish having actually got possession of the sugars, the noble author's argument comes four years too late: For, it has been plainly shewn to be the joint interest of planter, merchant, and consumer, to draw as many Sugars from the Irish as they possibly can.

Nevertheless the proposed measure, (not Lord North's measure, or Mr. Fox's measure) is to transfer (according to the noble author) not only the whole West India trade, but the American trade, and the tobacco trade too. But, by what means? The noble author conveys the whole mercantile capital of Europe to Ireland. In her Western ports the European traders, it seems, are to assemble; to build ships, where there are no wood or iron; to instruct the ignorant; to invigorate the indolent; and by a single movement to change the antient manners of a whole people.

But, to be serious (if it be possible when such arguments are brought forward on such an occasion;) it may be proper

per once more to remark, that though the mercantile capital both of Britain and Ireland are fast accumulating; the greatest capital, skill, and diligence must cause that capital to accumulate by the widest steps:—That Britain is in actual possession of the West India trade, the American trade, and the tobacco trade; of which she can not be deprived, unless she sits down, in security and idleness. But, he knows little of the world who thinks that the affairs of the world can ever stand still: mercantile capital must either be employed, or it must be realized. The British farmer must continue to follow the plow, the weaver must drive the shuttle, the sailor must set the sail, and the trader must actuate all.

In the West India trade England (exclusive of Scotland) has eight hundred vessels constantly employed, whose registered tonnage may be stated at a hundred thousand tons, but whose real burthen amounts to about one hundred and thirty thousand tons. When will Ireland possess such a West India fleet? She cannot buy the ships of America, Holland, or Hamburgh, because the act of navigation, being one of her fundamental laws, no more allows her, than it permits Britain, to own ships of foreign built. If she builds in Britain she will thereby promote a very valuable manufacture. And if she should build them at home she would by this means withdraw capital from some other branch of business, perhaps more beneficial to her and disadvantageous to this country. Till Ireland then shall have procured such a fleet, by whatever means, Britain must enjoy the freights both out and home. It is therefore in vain to say, that Ireland can victual and navigate cheaper than Britain, till she has vessels to victual. It is to as little purpose to argue against the most authentic facts, That her ports lying on the Atlantic Ocean must be nearer than those of England to the American coast; and that by this means, and the lowness of sailors wages she can perform the West India voyage at lower insurance and at cheaper freight: It is a well known fact, that the West India freights both out and home are constantly regulated by the mutual agreement of the traders and planters at satisfactory terms to both parties: It is a fact, that the insurers regarding the West India risques as desireable ones ask no higher premium either out or home, whether the ships call at Cork, or not: It is a fact too, that the freight and insurance from Cork are the same with those from London, whatever may be the greater speculative risque. The Irish
shipping

shipping cannot therefore enter into competition with the eight hundred ships beforementioned, which must necessarily go out for the sake of the homeward freights; and must therefore often go one half empty; since the whole cargoes outwards are not so bulky as one half of the cargoes homewards. Who then can seriously dread the rivalry of the Irish in respect to freights for ages to come? A little experience will teach the Irish, as it has already taught the British ship-owners, that capital cannot be employed in a less productive business, than it would be in owning West-India ships.

In soliciting consignments, the Irish will find great discouragements from being thus excluded from freights, which depend so much on interest and favour. But, there is in fact, such a chain of connexion, between the planter, merchant, and ship-master, wherein all their interests are bound, that it cannot be broken even by much greater advantages. The planter who has long consigned his sugars to his correspondent in London, or Bristol, will therefore continue to consign them still. The planter who resides in London, will not probably send his produce to Dublin for sale. Nor, will any planter, who knows, that in Ireland the West India products are sold in small quantities, on six months credit, while in Britain they are sold by the whole cargo, payable in two months, ever prefer that market, where there are the longest credits, and the greatest risques. It is said, though perhaps with some degree of exaggeration, that seven-eighths of the British West Indies belong, either mediately or immediately, to persons who reside in Britain. Were this fact true to a much smaller extent than is here represented, little sugar would ever be consigned to Ireland, because few men choose to send their property out of their sight, when they may have it to a greater advantage under their daily contemplation. A few cargoes have indeed been consigned from the West Indies to Ireland, during the last four years, by speculative men: But the account of sales were such, both as to price and payment, as not to countenance many repetitions of similar adventures.

If the proposed relaxation were granted to the desires of the Irish, it is apparent from the foregoing reasonings and facts, that Ireland must carry on the West India trade, however free, under every disadvantage. They would have as constant competitors the British traders, who have

greater

greater capitals and correspondence, who have established connexions and a wider market, and who are already in possession of the field of business. The Irish would have a competition both in the West-Indies and Europe, of a more dangerous kind: If the Irish, like the merchants of Glasgow, should be obliged for want of consignments and orders, to carry on this trade chiefly on their own account, they would have the English merchants for competitors in every market, as *factors*. And it requires no great knowledge to foretel, whether the *mere merchant*, or the *mere factor* would probably rise or fall, in carrying on such a traffick. With all these discouraging prospects before them, the Irish have made a beginning. In their small two decked vessels, they have sent to the West Indies provisions, and other products of pasturage, linen, and some lesser manufactures, to be sold at the best price on their own account. Every one must see, that this is a very hazardous trade: For, almost every article, which the Irish can bring, is imported by the planters for the supply of their own estates; who will only buy of them when it happens that their own stores have failed: The provisions, and other products of pasturage, are liable to a thousand accidents in a sultry climate. And the provision trade is therefore a most precarious trade, as we might infer from reason, if we had not experience to guide us.

But, when the Irish cargoes are all thus disposed of, another difficulty will immediately occur. The product of their sales will not be sufficient to buy more West India goods, considering their greater value, than will load the one half of the Irish vessels. They must draw bills for the balance that shall be wanting; for which they must find an indorser, at the expence of two and a half per cent. and which must be drawn on London, where all West India payments are made, or they will be charged two and a half per cent. more as the difference of exchange. Having brought the West India goods, loaded with all these disadvantages, to Ireland, the Irish trader will there meet the British merchants as competitors, who may have brought similar cargoes directly from the West Indies, or indirectly from Britain.

Owing to the difficulties before-mentioned the Irish have yet made no great progress during the five years freedom of their West India trade; as we may observe from the following statement *:

* Irish Cust. Houf Accounts.

A comparative account of the sugar and rum, which were imported into Ireland, during the subjoined years, ending the 25th March,

Sugars Muscavado.

	1781 cwt.	1782 cwt.	1783 cwt.	1784 cwt.
From the West-Indies	130,056	132,754	99,240	160,083
From Britain	7,384	18,683	33,870	27,492

Rum.

	1781 gal.	1782 gal.	1783 gal.	1784 gal.
From the West-Indies	69,473	175,053	297,047	153,592
From Britain	197,832	99,219	129,951	944,479

Sugar and rum may be regarded as the representatives of the West-India products for the purpose of this comparison. The importations from Britain were probably somewhat affected by the Irish distractions. It is surely reasonable to infer, from the foregoing facts and arguments, that the importations to Ireland will continue nearly in this state for half a century to come. It is obvious however, that Ireland must supply her own consumption, before she can smuggle or send any sugars to Britain. And when in the long progress of her trade she shall have any surplus to spare such sugars must be sent to Britain loaded with an additional expence of 3s. 6d. to 4s. per cwt. including Custom-house fees, insurance, freight and factorage.

How far the allowing of the importation of these surplus sugars in British ships would give the American commerce to Ireland, is a question which may now be easily answered. We may all remember the prophecies that were uttered, as to the loss of that trade from the revolt of the colonies first, and from the independence of the United States afterwards. We have all seen the race which was run soon after that event, by the commercial nations of Europe for the golden prize of the American trade. While the contest was yet undecided, it was insisted on behalf of the ultimate success of Britain: That the skill and capital of the British manufacturers were such as to enable them to give the American traders better pennyworths and longer credits than any other tradesmen in Europe: And that the Americans,

Americans, being at once regardful of their interest and in want of capital, would necessarily come to the warehouse where they could get the best and cheapest goods, with the longest time to pay for them. No one urged these and similar reasonings with more efficacy than Lord Sheffield, in a pamphlet, which gained him some praise, by entailing on Britain the American trade: It is only to be lamented, that the noble author should have so soon found cause to dock the entail, and to settle the American commerce on Ireland. The event of the before-mentioned race is now universally known. Britain has engrossed the American trade to a degree which is almost beyond belief. The Spanish merchants who engaged in the American trade, have failed. The French American merchants have failed. A few British merchants have failed. And have the Irish had no failures among the traders who engaged in the American commerce?

Experience hath now determined several doubtful points, in our commercial concerns, that no argument could have done. It was foretold, that the French would, from the revolt, engross the whole tobacco of Virginia and Maryland. Yet, though the farmers-general sent a proper agent to Virginia, who has also failed, and though they are supported by the public money; they are now buying tobacco in London. And is it likely, that the Irish can engross the whole tobacco trade, greatly inferior as they are even to the French in opulence and skill, activity and address? The Irish have not yet supplied their own wants: Till they acquire all these qualities in a higher degree, they cannot supply the wants of others with any foreign product. It is London, which, from the vastness of her market for every luxurious and every useful article of traffick, must for ages be the American mart, without some accident that no sagacity can foresee, or prudence prevent.

But, it is still pertinaciously urged, that by granting this boon to the Irish, we should relinquish *the monopoly* of the plantation trade, which was confined to Britain by the Act of Navigation. This had doubtless been an objection, though not a weighty one, to Lord North's concessions of the colony trade to Ireland: But, this can be no objection to allowing British subjects to import in British ships from Ireland to Britain such surplusses of American products as had not been consumed by her. It was doubted formerly by some, whether this monopoly ought to be considered as an evil, or a good: That it is an evil rather than a good,

has

has been shewn very clearly by Dr. Adam Smith. Every monopoly is said to be more favourable to the few, than to the many: By yielding a greater profit to those who are favoured by it than they otherwise would gain, the monopoly, it is argued, forces a greater portion of mercantile capital within its operation, than otherwise would go there: That by this means, capital is often withdrawn from domestic manufactures, or from a neighbouring trade of Europe into a more distant commerce, which is less under our eye: That of consequence the monopoly of the plantation trade oppressed every other commercial business which was unconnected with it: And that by these operations, the American trade became a disease in our commercial policy, like those unnatural tumours in the human body, which often occasion lameness and death. The American trade formerly, and the plantation trade now, are certainly very advantageous to this kingdom: It is only doubted whether the *monopoly* of that trade, which is a distinct thing, be a desireable object.

But, let us suppose, in opposition to these reasonings and to that authority, that the monopoly is a good rather than an evil, it may be worth while to enquire, whether Ireland was originally excluded from it by the Act of Navigation. The great object of this famous law was to exclude, alien men and foreign ships from trading with our colonies. This regulation was plainly intended for the benefit of every part of the dominions of the crown: The colonies were allowed to trade with each other: Ireland was in the same manner admitted by the Act of Navigation * itself to the most unlimitted freedom of trade, with all the plantations, till afterwards excluded, more by private resentment † than by public policy. The continental colonies from the epoch to the period of the revolt were allowed to carry sugar from the British West-Indies into their own ports and to send them from thence to England. From the act of the 23d Charles II. Ireland could not import

---

* See 12 Cha. ch. 18.

† The revenge of St. John for an affront in Holland is said to have given rise to the Act of Navigation, during the Commonwealth: It was in the same manner, the individual resentment of the profligate Shaftsbury against the virtuous Ormond, who then governed Ireland, that gave rise to almost all the restrictions of the Irish trade, during Charles IId's reign, some of which appear at present perfectly ridiculous. [See Hume's History of that period.]

APPENDIX. 51

port Sugars from the plantations, and consequently was not permitted to send sugars from her own ports to Britain. The colonies which were thus allowed this right maintained no military establishment: Ireland who was denied this right did maintain a military establishment, which was applied to the general defence. The colonies, which were thus indulged, have always required an enormous expence to defend them: Ireland, who was thus excluded, has occasioned no particular expence; at least peaceable Ireland has not, whatever distracted Ireland may have done. New Brunswick and Nova Scotia, may even now re-export British sugars to Britain, yet Britain pays their civil lists. But, Ireland, who pays her own civil lists and supports moreover a great army, is denied this convenience. If this conduct was unequal and unjust formerly, can the continuance of a similar conduct be wise and equitable now? Thus Ireland was entitled originally to all the benefits of monopoly; and is even now entitled to all the benefits of the monopoly, except the convenience of re-shipping British sugars in British ships to Britain; the denial of which is not of any great consequence to this country, whatever it may be to her.

2. From the foregoing considerations we are led secondly to enquire, whether the proposed indulgence has any tendency to impugn or weaken that principle of the Navigation Act, which has certainly created so many shipping and seamen, the more valuable, as they belong to ourselves. If the proposal were to allow *foreign* ships to bring the surplus sugars of Ireland to Britain, the circumstance of their being foreign ships and seamen would be a decisive objection. Were it proposed to confine the bringing over such sugars to ships, merely Irish; which had not been often declared by law, and admitted in fact to be British vessels; this circumstance had created a considerable objection. But the shipping and sailors intended by the proposal, being British shipping and sailors, without exception, the proposal can surely be liable to no great objection.

If therefore the proposal should be adopted, and in consequence thereof many surplusses should be sent, more native sailors should thereby be employed; and the principle of the Act of Navigation would therefore be strengthened: If, on the other hand, it is probable, that few or no sugars will be sent from Ireland in half a century, then the object is not worth a contest.

The

The trade between the sister kingdoms has grown up in less than a century, from the lowest state of depression, owing to the restrictions of the reign of Charles II. to a very high point of magnitude, owing to our having gradually removed those restrictions. We shall see this important truth in a very clear light from the following statement:

	Value of Exports.	Value of Imports.
The amount of the trade between England and Ireland, according to a three years average ending with 1695 was	£. 166,025	81,165
Ditto ending with 1783 was	1,873,236	1,427,191

It plainly required no great number of ships to carry on the trade between the sister kingdoms, during King William's reign: And this trade certainly furnished very few seamen for the royal navy, during King William's wars, when they were so much wanted. It is equally apparent, that it must have employed many ships to transport the vast cargoes of the years 1781-2-3: And it is equally plain, that the navigation, which was thus created, must have furnished many seamen for the public service, during our late unhappy contests. Both the trade and the nursery seem to be a new creation, since the beginning of the present century. If this creation was so much gain to the nation, with a view to its defence, to extend this creation still further, with the same most important end, must be a good to be desired; and to depress that creation, or narrow that nursery, must be an evil to be avoided.

If we have the wisdom, and the equity to open the ports of Ireland still wider, by granting the little that is now desired, we shall certainly strengthen the principle of the navigation act, by increasing the number of ships, and consequently, the number of *native* seamen; which the Irish have been declared by law, and are acknowledged in fact to be. In proportion then as we shut the Irish ports, we enfeeble the salutary principle of the navigation act, by doing that which must necessarily lessen the number of seamen, who may be most easily engaged when they are very much wanted.

By

APPENDIX. 53

By thus promoting the public service, Bristol, Liverpool, and Whitehaven have surely nothing to fear on the subject of freights: For, their great numbers of return ships, stand a much better chance for employment than any Irish ships, which may be chartered on purpose: The vessels which must necessarily return home, can afford to carry at a lower freight, than a vessel which must fit out only for a single voyage: And consequently the British ship owners must overpower the Irish in every competition for freights; which must necessarily augment the number of British ships, without diminishing the actual number of Irish.

On the other hand, were the re-shipping of sugars, as hath been proposed, to augment the number of seamen in the ports of Ireland, without diminishing the number of vessels in the ports of England, because the present trade would probably continue as to them, while the advantage in the competition shall continue, nothing would surely tend so much to promote the public service, during our wars, as having a great number of sailors, who are bound to serve, in the ports of Limerick and Cork, Waterford and Dublin: For these ports being nearer to Plymouth and Portsmouth, than Liverpool or Lancaster, Whitehaven, or Greenock, the supernumerary sailors of the Irish ports beforementioned could be more conveniently commanded than from the more distant British ports. The same observation equally applies to the whole navigation between the sister kingdoms, as compared with longer voyages. In short voyages the sailors often return into port, and may therefore often be had: In more distant voyages the seamen seldom return, and consequently can seldom be engaged in the public service, when this service may very much require their aid.

It was with a view to the usefulness of these repeated voyages, between neighbouring harbours, that the navigation act excluded by an express clause, alien ships and sailors from carrying any merchandize from one port to another, in England and Ireland, or from these kingdoms to the circumjacent British Islands. The navigation act then considered the home trade of Ireland as part of the coast trade of England, which has been so carefully preserved as the most valuable nursery for seamen. And indeed what can the whole navigation between the sister kingdoms be deemed, but a coast trade, which ought to

H be

be extended by every rational measure that can be proposed or thought of. Foreigners were excluded too from the trade of the Colonies upon the principle *of keeping up a firmer connexion between the parent country and them.* Let us hope, that by granting the enlargement of navigation, which is now desired by the Irish, it may be the efficacious means of strengthening the union between the sister kingdoms, which is so much for the interest and happiness of both.

3. From considerations with regard to the naval strength of the empire, it is proper to inquire briefly, in the third place, as to the question, how far the public burdens of this country would be lightened at present, or lessened in future, were the Irish proposals adopted.

The revenue of every country is divided in modern times, into two kinds; 1st, the income of every individual separately, from whatever means: 2dly, the income of all the individuals collectively, which is called the public revenue, on the income of the state. The private revenue of no country on earth ever accumulated faster than the private revenue of this kingdom, during the last hundred years, which continues to accumulate abundantly at this moment. But, the public revenue, however great and productive it may be under late management, is depressed by many debts, funded and unfunded. It is apparent therefore, that the wisdom of our counsels ought to be chiefly occupied in strengthening the public revenue, which is thus feeble; leaving private incomes which are thus productive to the care of individuals, who are entitled to general protection, without the particular interference of the state.

It is to be lamented, how often the spirit of the people is directed to improper objects. They have been well nigh ruined, in their public revenue, by being induced to clamour for commercial advantages. We were so absurd as to settle colonies for the sake of getting a nation of customers. We have spent hundreds of millions to enlarge and defend distant dominions to enjoy those commercial advantages, which experience hath shewn are best enjoyed without any public expence. Yet, the same man, who by his misconduct and mistakes, has almost beggared his country, in pursuit of the phantom of commercial advantages, continues to insist, that we ought to risque our all, in pursuit of commercial advantages.

While

APPENDIX. 55

While this nation conftantly grafped at a fhadow, almoft every foreign power has been acquiring provinces which have yielded *public* revenue. But what has Britain gained even from her moft fuccefsful wars? She acquired diftant deferts which were difadvantageous to this as an induftrious and mercantile country, in two refpects; 1ft. Inftead of yielding *public* revenue they required *public* fupport at no fmall expence for civil and military eftablifhments; 2dly, Commercial capital was conftantly withdrawn from domeftic induftry, wherein it was employed to the greateft advantage, to cultivate deferts beyond the ocean, without adequate returns. With our fad experience and prefent knowledge we may eafily determine the queftion, whether we ought to accept of any diftant ifland, or country, however large, were it offered without any equivalent? For, we have feen, that it would require a civil lift or government to be paid from the public revenue, which cannot be fpared; and that it would drain the people of the mercantile capital which now gives employment to every induftrious individual.

On the other hand, Ireland is directly the reverfe of fuch an ifland, inhabited as Ireland already is, by a numerous people, brave, active and generous; who, at the annual expence of a million, fupport a great civil and military eftablifhment; and who, without any apparent diminution of our capitals, are our yearly cuftomers to the amount of nearly two millions. In fuperaddition to thefe great advantages, which ought to be regarded as no fmall equivalents for commercial benefits, Ireland propofes to appropriate the furpluffes of the hereditary revenue, as a fund for the more general purpofe of protecting the Empire.

We ought to inquire into the nature and extent of this revenue before we determine, whether it is worth our acceptance. It confifts then of a Cuftom-houfe duty, outwards and inwards, of an inland and inward excife; and of a tax, called hearth-money. It is obvious, that thefe taxes are of fuch a nature as to have increafed and to continue to increafe with the populoufnefs, the induftry, the trade, and opulence of the country. We have already feen how vaftly the trade of Ireland has grown fince the Revolution in 1688. And from the following ftatement we may have a very diftinct view of the increafe of the hereditary revenue from that æra to the prefent time:

This revenue produced then, according
to a five years average, ending with   1687 £.231,780
Ditto ending with   -   1734   .300,332
Ditto ending with   -   -   -   1753   417,000
A seven years average ending with   -   1770   545,422
Ditto   ending with   1777   543,818
The year ending with Lady Day   1784   659,000

A real statesman would desire no better document than this to judge of the progress in population, diligence, traffick, and wealth of any people. A real statesman when he considered from what funds this increasing revenue arose and how fast it had augmented, during a century of oppression, would easily determine with regard to the rapidity wherewith the same revenue must hereafter increase from the epoch of the freedom of Ireland, both commercial and political.

It is a curious fact in the history of our parties and debts, that when Walpole *established the sinking fund*, it became immediately the subject of ridicule to the fashionable orators and wits of the times. Yet, every one knows, that the sinking fund which when created in 1717 did not yield half so great a sum as the hereditary revenue of Ireland, produced in 1781 rather more than three million, till it was almost dissipated by the unproductive taxes of a great financier, for which it was security. Ridicule therefore is not always the test of truth.

He must indeed have little wit and less wisdom, who can suppose, that the hereditary revenue, whatever may be its produce, is the only public income, which Ireland contributes for defraying the expence of defending the empire, of which Ireland forms so great a part. Ireland maintains as great a land army as Britain does. The military establishments of the sister kingdoms form the military defence of each other. One Generalissimo commands both, who may direct the operations of both for the protection of each. If Ireland maintained fewer troops, Britain must maintain more: If Ireland supported none, Britain must double hers. The reduction of military establishments of every kind is in the present state of the revenue of Britain perhaps the best œconomy. If Ireland, by maintaining her military establishment to the full extent, facilitates this reduction and œconomy in favour of Britain she thereby contributes positive income. In this manner do foreign powers calculate the conjoint forces of the sister kingdoms. It can never be prudent in either to convince the world, by unreasonable desires on either side, that we are a divided people, whose armies are separate, and whose interests are distinct.

We all remember how much it has been regretted, that the Congress petition, which was delivered by Mr. Penn, was not received and considered as the beginning of reconcilement. But, the authority of the Congress was disputed by some, and their terms were regarded by many as designedly general and studiously subtle. On the other hand, the Irish proposals come from the only power which could legally send them; and these proposals are detailed into such distinct resolutions, that their meaning is obvious and their purposes plainly avowed. Let us not have it to lament hereafter, that we opposed such proposals captiously, much less that we rejected them hastily.

Whoever recollects what distraction prevailed in Ireland only a twelvemonth ago, and compares them with the present repose, must be of opinion, that much has been skilfully done. To obtain such proposals, from such an authority, with the declared intention of finally settling the commercial affairs of the sister kingdoms, on liberal principles of mutual advantage, was doubtless to advance many steps towards a desirable object. Let us be cautious how we undo that which has already been done; far less how we by any means drive Ireland into fresh distractions, in quest of old remedies, and new pretensions. It cannot surely be the interest of any class of men among us, to see agreements of non-importation again entered into by the Irish populace, or protecting duties once more imposed by the Irish parliament. The manufactures ought to recollect, how much they were baffled by such agreements before: The merchants would do well to remember, a recent example of commercial connexions of great extent, being wholly cut off by by such associations alone. Every wise man must be of opinion, that peaceful and industrious Ireland is a mine of riches, and a tower of strength to Britain: That distracted Ireland would be her weakness in war, and her bane in peace. To prevent such apprehensions in future, these proposals have

been

been submitted to parliament, only as part of a plan of systematic government, which can alone tie the sister kingdoms more closely together. The adoption of this plan bids fair to insure mutual confidence, and lasting good will. The rejection of these proposals would lead to ills that cannot all be foreseen, but would be all deplored hereafter.

APPENDIX.

CONSIDERATIONS

RESPECTING THE

Proposed Arrangements with IRELAND.

THE home market is limitted in every country to the number of its inhabitants: But foreign trade hath the world for its customer in sales and purchases, where a large capital necessarily producing low interest at home, enables the exporting merchant of a rich country, to give a longer credit for what he sells, than the merchant of a poor country can give. Thus circumstanced, it is unnecessary to say who will have the preference.

In like manner the profits upon what both purchase at the same rate will be greater, in proportion to the difference of interest. Half per cent. will turn the scale of commerce; such in that single article, with an addition at least of half per cent. more, will be the comparative state of Great-Britain and Ireland, at their first setting out, under the proposed regulations; while, if their returns be at equal periods, one per cent. profit, added at every return to the British capital, and operating in trade as interest upon interest, will be in favour of Great-Britain, added to her superior skill in manufacture, the general use of engines which shorten labour, and must, when ever generally used in Ireland, be purchased at a great expence, deducted from her small capital, the possession of correspondence long tried, the habits of being supplied with long accustomed articles for wear and other purposes, or the love of variety, which may now be incomparably better gratified by Britain, connected with the solid advantage of a long credit. These are some of the circumstances which must be overcome by Ireland, before her prosperity can be an object of apprehension to her sister kingdom; yet as has been observed by the author of a late pamphlet, in countries circumstanced as these are, the richest will ever preserve its superiority.

But if Ireland should gradually increase, as we hope she will, and the faster she grows the better it will be for us; nay, if all the markets of the known world were now sufficiently stocked, France, mistress of a smaller capital than ours

ours in foreign trade, and far from being equal to us in the most profitable manufactures, is more valuable than we are by Irish rivalship.

That the Turkey trade for lower priced cloths, much the most valuable branch, because the most in demand there, though lost to us and gained to France, would, in a great measure, be supported by Ireland, is proved by a well-known fact, that during the prohibition of exporting woollens from thence, the French assortments were not only, in a great degree, made of Irish wool, manufactured in France, but of cloths smuggled from Ireland with the risk of capture upon them; nor was this the worst effect of that tyrannical prohibition; France stood indebted to it for the first rise of her woollen manufactures, even for her own consumption. Yet the authors of that cruel measure, and the English manufacturers who urged them to it, foretold it would secure to England the woollen trade of the universe: So it stands recorded in the annals of William III. and should now be perused as a warning to the nation and its ministers, against predictions suggested by ignorant and narrow-minded manufacturers, who consider Ireland as their sole competitor, and, with the spirit of a village smith, who shut out his neighbouring brother of the anvil, as a foreigner, would in like manner exclude Ireland.

Such is more particularly the spirit of that petition against admitting her to our market for cottons, while it is known that great quantities are run, particularly from Dieppe, and sold in London.

This is no secret to the Lancashire Petitioners, and would furnish a strong argument for the reduction of duties laid upon their manufacture. But as it would militate still stronger in favour of Ireland; the fact, though lately vehemently complained of, is now cautiously withheld in silence and secrecy.

We cannot help here taking notice of the peculiar modesty of Mr. Peel's proposition to protect ourselves against the importation of Irish cottons, by a duty of thirty-three per cent. which implies a tax to that amount upon the British wearer of cottons, for the exclusive benefit of Manchester.

March 22, 1785.

Forgery

This Day is published by JOHN STOCKDALE, opposite Burlington-House, Piccadilly.

SHAKSPEARE.

Printed from the Text of SAMUEL JOHNSON and GEORGE STEEVENS, Esq. In one large Volume octavo. On a fine Royal Paper, and embellished with a striking likeness of the Author,

Price 15s. in boards.
   17s. 6d. bound in calf and lettered.
   18s. elegantly bound in calf and gilt.
   19s. neatly bound in Russia leather, gilt.
   1l. 1s. beautifully bound in vellum, gilt.
   1l. 5s. bound in Morocco, extra.
And 3l. 3s. bound in tortoiseshell.

STOCKDALE's EDITION

OF

SHAKSPEARE,

INCLUDING THE WHOLE OF HIS

DRAMATIC WORKS;

Compiled from VARIOUS COMMEN-TATORS.

" Nature her pencil to his hand commits,
And then in all her forms to this great Master fits."
            ADDRESS

BOOKS printed for JOHN STOCKDALE.

ADDRESS TO THE PUBLIC.

A new edition of SHAKSPEARE, and an edition of so singular a form as the present, in which all his plays are comprehended in one volume, will, perhaps, appear surprising to many readers; but, upon a little reflection, their surprise will, the Editor doubts not, be converted into approbation.

Much as SHAKSPEARE has been read of late years, and largely as the admiration and study of him have been extended, there is still a numerous class of men to whom he is imperfectly known. Many of the middling and lower ranks of the inhabitants of this country are either not acquainted with him at all, excepting by name, or have only seen a few of his plays, which have accidentally fallen in their way. It is to supply the wants of these persons that the present Edition is principally undertaken; and it cannot fail of becoming to them a perpetual source of entertainment and instruction. That they will derive the highest entertainment from it, no one can deny; for it does not require any extraordinary degree of knowledge or education to enter into the general spirit of SHAKSPEARE. The passions he describes are the passions which are felt by every human being; and his wit and humour are not local, or confined to the customs of a particular age, but are such as will give pleasure at all times, and to men of all ranks, from the highest to the lowest.

But the instruction that may be drawn from SHAKSPEARE is equal to the entertainment which his writings afford. He is the greatest master of human nature, and of human life, that, perhaps, ever existed; so that we cannot peruse his works without having our understandings considerably enlarged. Besides this, he abounds in occasional maxims and reflections, which are calculated to make a deep impression upon the mind. There is scarcely any circumstance in the common occurrences of the world, on which something may not be found peculiarly applicable in SHAKSPEARE; and at the same time, better expressed than in any other author. To promote, therefore, knowledge of him, is to contribute to the general improvement.

Nor is the utility of the present publication confined to persons of the rank already described; it will be found serviceable to those whose situations in life have enabled them

BOOKS printed for JOHN STOCKDALE.

to purchafe all the expenfive editions of our great dramatift. The book now offered to the public may commodioufly be taken into a coach or poft chaife, for amufement in a journey; or if a company of gentlemen fhould happen, in converfation, to mention SHAKSPEARE, or to difpute concerning any particular paffage, a volume, containing the whole of his plays may, with great convenience be fetched by a fervant out of a library or clofet. In fhort, any particular paffage may, at all times, and with eafe, be recurred to. It is a compendium, not an abridgement, of the nobleft of our poets, and a library in a fingle volume.

The Editor hath endeavoured to give all the perfection to this work which the nature of it can admit. The account of his life, which is taken from Rowe, and his laft will, in reality, comprehend almoft every thing that is known with regard to the perfonal hiftory of SHAKSPEARE. The anxious refearches of his admirers have fcarcely been able to collect any farther information concerning him.

The text in the prefent edition, has been given as it was fettled by the moft approved commentators. It does not confift with the limits of the defign, that the notes fhould be large, or very numerous: they have not, however, been wholly neglected. The notes which are fubjoined are fuch as were neceffary for the purpofe of illuftrating and explaining obfolete words, unufual phrafes, old cuftoms, and obfcure or diftant allufions. In fhort, it has been the Editor's aim to omit nothing which may ferve to render SHAKSPEARE intelligible to every capacity, and to every clafs of readers.

Having this view, he cannot avoid expreffing his hope, that an undertaking, the utility of which is fo apparent, will be encouraged by the public; and his confidence of a favourable reception is increafed by the confcioufnefs that he is not doing an injury to any one. The fuccefs of the prefent volume will not impede the fale of the larger editions of SHAKSPEARE, which will ftill be equally fought for by thofe to whom the purchafe of them may be convenient.

☞ Gentlemen in the Country finding a difficulty in procuring the above valuable Work, by directing a Line to Mr. STOCKDALE, oppofite Burlington Houfe, Piccadilly, appointing the Payment thereof in London, fhall have it immediately forwarded, carriage paid, to any Part of Great Britain.

NEW PAMPHLETS, printed for JOHN STOCKDALE, Piccadilly, for the Year 1785.

A DIALOGUE between a JUSTICE of the PEACE and a FARMER. By Thomas Day, Efq; Price 3s.

A LETTER to the JURORS of GREAT BRITAIN. By George Rous, Efq; Price 2s.

EVERY MAN HIS OWN LAW-MAKER; or, The Englifhman's Complete Guide to a Parliamentary Reform: Wherein the Road to National Confufion is made plain and eafy to the meaneft capacities. Price 1s.

——————————— For I
At firft was mine own king———
    Caliban in the Tempeft, Act I.

The EMPEROR's CLAIMS. Being a Defcription of the City of ANTWERP, and the River SCHELDE; with a concife Hiftory of the AUSTRIAN NETHERLANDS: Together with Extracts from the Articles of the Treaty of Munfter, and thofe of the Barrier Treaty, whereby the Dutch found their right to the blocking up of the Schelde. Adorned with an elegant Map of the River Schelde; a View of the City of Antwerp, and all the adjacent Imperial and Dutch Territories, neatly coloured. Dedicated to the EMPEROR. Price 2s. 6d.

The

New Books printed for John Stockdale.

The IDEA of a PATRIOT CITIZEN, or TRUE REFORM; in a Letter to a Noble Lord. Price 1s. 6d.

ENGLAND's ALARM! on the prevailing Doctrine of LIBELS, as laid down by the Earl of Mansfield.

> 'Twill be *recorded* for a *precedent*;
> And *many* an *error*, by the *same example*,
> Will *rush* into the *State*—IT CANNOT BE.
> SHAKSPEARE.

In a Letter to his Lordship. By a Country Gentleman. To which is added, by way of Appendix, the celebrated Dialogue between a Gentleman and a Farmer. Written by Sir William Jones; with Remarks thereon, and on the Cafe of the Dean of St. Afaph. Price 1s. 6d.

The DEFORMITY of the DOCTRINE of LIBELS, and Informations *Ex Officio*, with a View of the Cafe of the Dean of St. Afaph, and an Enquiry into the Rights of Jurymen, in a Letter to the Honourable Thomas Erfkine. By M. Dawes, Efq; Price 1s.

A PLAN for finally fettling the Government of Ireland upon Conftitutional Principles; and the chief Caufe of the unprofperous State of that Country explained. Price 1s. 6d.

New Books printed for JOHN STOCKDALE.

POLITICAL LETTERS, written in March and April 1784. Price 2s.
†+† Be careful to afk for that printed for Stockdale.

STRICTURES upon NAVAL DEPARTMENTS, &c. &c. Price 2s.

The COALITION RENCONTRE ANTICIPATED. A Poetical Dialogue. With a Frontifpiece. Price 2s.

KINGWESTON HILL, a Poem. Price 1s. 6d.

An ELEGY to the Memory of Dr. Samuel Johnfon. By Thomas Hobhoufe, Efq; Price 6d.

The LONDON KALENDAR, or Court and City Regifter for the Year 1785. Price 2s.

Including all the new Peers lately created; new Members; alterations in the different Departments under Government in Great Britain, Ireland, and America; with a complete Lift of the Sovereigns of Europe; the Prefidents of the Congrefs from 1774; Prefidents and Governors of the American States; and a number of other new Lifts, not to be found in any other Publication. Containing complete Lifts of the Britifh and Irifh Houfes of Parliament; Eftablifhments of England, Scotland, Ireland, and America, &c. Correct Lifts of the Peereffes, Baronets, Univerfities, Seminaries, Hofpitals, Charities, Governors, Public Offices; Army, Navy, Collectors at the different Ports, &c.

This

New Books printed for John Stockdale.

This London Kalendar is upon a plan much more extensive and useful, than any other Book of the kind yet published.

✝✝✝ Be careful to ask for the London Kalendar printed for J. STOCKDALE, &c.

STOCKDALE's NEW COMPANION to the LONDON KALENDAR: or COURT AND CITY REGISTER, for the year 1785: Being a List of all Changes in Administration, from the accession of the present King, in October 1760, to the present time. To which are prefixed, Lists of the two last and present Parliaments; shewing the changes made by the General Elections in 1780 and 1784; with the Names of the Candidates where the Elections were contested, and the numbers polled; also the dates when each city and borough first sent Representatives to Parliament, the right of election in each select place, and the supposed number of voters.

To this edition is added, a summary account of the duties of the great Officers of State: a table of the duration of the several Parliaments, from Henry VII. to the present time: a List of those places which formerly sent Members to Parliament, and now do not; a List of the Deaths of the principal Ministers during the present reign. With an APPENDIX, containing the Cases of controverted Elections, as they lately appeared before several Committees; with their Determination thereupon; and a complete Index of Names. Price 1s. 6d.

✝✝✝ Be careful to ask for STOCKDALE's New Companion, which may be had separate, or bound with the London Kalendar.

New Books printed for John Stockdale.

COMMITTEE RESOLVES.

Price THREE SHILLING AND SIXPENCE in Boards,

THE RESOLVES OF THE COMMITTEE appointed to try the Merits of the ELECTION for the COUNTY of GLOUCESTER, in the Year 1777.

GEORGE BERKELEY, Efq. Petitioner.

WM. BROMLEY CHESTER, Efq. Sitting Member.

The above Resolves are faithfully extracted from Manuscript Notes of the Proceedings of the Committee, taken at the Time,

By SIR CECIL WRAY, Bart.

The following are the Gentlemen who composed the Committee, which began to sit the 5th of February, and continued till the 29th of April; in the course of which time there were near one hundred Divisions upon particular Votes.

Sir CECIL WRAY, Bart. Chairman.

John Elwes, and Geo. Johnstone, Esqrs. Nominees.

Sir Wm. Cunnyngham, Bart.	Sir Geo. Robinson, Bart.
C. A. Pelham, Efq.	Hugh Owen, Efq.
Thomas Powys, Efq.	Hon. Charles Finch.
Edward Phelips, Efq.	Charles Penruddock, Efq.
Thomas Brand, Efq.	Edward Morant, Efq.
John Cleveland, Efq.	John Halliday, Efq.

NEW

NEW BOOKS printed for JOHN STOCKDALE.

DEBATES of the laſt SESSION of the late PARLIAMENT; including, amongſt a variety of other important and intereſting Matter, a complete and particular Account of the whole of the Debates on the ſeveral great Queſtions that led to the Diſſolution, followed up to the Day on which it took Place, conſtituting one of the moſt Capital Details of Parliamentary Information ever known: including the whole of the Proceedings of the St. Alban's Tavern Meeting, correct Liſts of the Diviſions, and of the whole Houſe, as it ſtood the Day it was diſſolved, ſhewing how each Member divided.

In 6 Vols. 8vo. Price 1l. 10s. in Boards.

N. B. Nothing can be more neceſſary than theſe Debates, not only for the new Members, but for all thoſe who ſat in the laſt Houſe of Commons, as well on Account of the Hiſtory contained in them of the greateſt Political Events that ever agitated this Country, as their ſhewing the State in which a variety of Buſineſs was left at the Diſſolution of Parliament, which will be taken up again and reconſidered b- the new Houſe of Commons.

⁎ Thoſe Gentlemen who have had part of the above Work are requeſted to complete it as ſoon as poſſible.

A SHORT ADDRESS to the diſintereſted and unprejudiced Citizens, Merchants and Manufacturers of Great Britain, on the Importance of the Trade of this Country, with the United States of America; alſo reaſons why, as Cuſtomers, they ſhould not be reſtricted, like other Foreign Nations, from ſending Raw Materials to this Country in Payment of Britiſh Goods. Price One Shilling.

By A MANUFACTURER.

An AUTHENTIC COPY of the JUDGEMENT delivered by the Right Honourable Earl Manſfield, November the 16th, 1784, in the Caſe of the King againſt William Davies Shipley, Dean of St. Aſaph. Price One Shilling.

NEW

New Books printed for JOHN STOCKDALE.

PARLIAMENTARY GUIDE.

In One Large Volume Octavo, containing upwards of Five Hundred Pages, Price Seven Shillings in Boards,

STOCKDALE's

PARLIAMENTARY GUIDE;

OR,

MEMBERS' AND ELECTORS'

COMPLETE COMPANION:

Being an HISTORICAL ACCOUNT of the several CITIES, COUNTIES, and BOROUGHS, in GREAT-BRITAIN; their Right of Election: when they were first represented in Parliament, and the Number of Voters at each Place; with References to the Journals of the House of Commons, for every Proceeding to be found in them relating to Matters of Election; and Copies of the several Writs used at a General Re-election; the Oaths taken by the Electors and the Elected, and the Oaths administered to the Representative upon taking his Seat; with a full Recitation of all the various Statutes relating to the Election of Members, and the Succession of Parliaments from the Restoration.

To which is prefixed,

A PREFACE,

Digested under the Seven following Heads, viz.

The Origin of Parliament, its Progress, and Present State—Observations on the last General Writ—Original Mode of Election—How the Rights of Election have been preserved—Of the Constitution of Committees for trying controverted Elections; the Manner of proceeding in them, and Regulations concerning the same—The Number of Members returned in the different Reigns---and Observations on the present Work.

WITH

AN APPENDIX,

Containing Orders of the House of Commons, arranged under their proper Heads; and a Table of Fees taken by its Officers and Servants.

New Books printed for JOHN STOCKDALE.

Elegantly printed in Three Volumes, 8vo. Price 18s. Half Bound and Lettered,

THE

DEBATES

AND

PROCEEDINGS

OF THE

HOUSE OF COMMONS,

DURING THE

FIRST SESSION OF THE SIXTEENTH PARLIAMENT

OF

GREAT BRITAIN.

THE PUBLISHER returns his sincere Thanks to those numerous Gentlemen (Members of Parliament and Others) who

New Books printed for John Stockdale.

who have so kindly aided him in the Completion of this useful and accurate Detail of the Proceedings in the last Session of Parliament. He will not presume to enter into any Commendation of them, fully convinced that their own Merit, from the Accuracy with which they have been taken, and the Attention given them, will sufficiently recommend them to his numerous Friends and the Public in general.

London, Feb. 5, 1785.

www.ingramcontent.com/pod-product-compliance
Lightning Source LLC
Chambersburg PA
CBHW020127170426
43199CB00009B/677